Modern Wood Turning

Other Drake Woodworking Books

Artistry in Wood	M. Vincent Hayes
Built-ins for Home Improvement	James E. Waters
Cabinets and Built-ins	Charles H. Hayward
Carpenters' Tools: Their Care and Maintenance	Charles H. Hayward
Cabinet Making For Beginners	Charles H. Hayward
The Complete Handyman	Charles H. Hayward
The Complete Book of Woodwork	Charles H. Hayward
The Encyclopedia of Furniture Making	Ernest Joyce
Furniture, Furniture Finishing, Decoration and Patching	Albert Brace Pattou and Clarence Lee Vaughn
Introducing Furniture Making	John R. Trussell
Introducing Marquetry	Marie Campkin
Loudspeakers and Loudspeaker Cabinets	P. W. Van Der Wal
Making Toys in Wood	Charles H. Hayward
Practical Upholstery	C. Howes
Making Wooden Toys	Michael Fletcher
The Practical Wood Turner	F. Pain
Staining and Polishing	Charles H. Hayward
Timbers for Woodwork	J. C. S. Brough
Wood Finishing — Plain and Decorative	F. N. Vanderwalker
The Woodblock Engravers	Kenneth Lindley
Woodwork Joints	Charles H. Hayward
Violin Making: As It Was and Is	Ed. by Heron-Allen
Woodcarving	Charles H. Hayward and William Wheeler

Modern Wood Turning

Gordon Stokes

Drake Publishers Inc   New York

ISBN 87749–295–6

Published in 1973 by
Drake Publishers Inc
381 Park Avenue South
New York, N.Y.10016

Printed in Great Britain

Contents

Suppliers of Lumber and Equipment

Albert Constantine and Sons, Inc.
2050 Eastchester Road
Bronx, N.Y. 10461

Minnesota Woodworkers Supply Co.
925 Winnetka Avenue North
Minneapolis, Minnesota 55427

Cummings Wood Co.
30 Bartholemew Avenue
Hartford, Connecticut 06106

Advance Process Supply Co.
400 North Noble Street
Chicago, Illinois 60622

Craftsman Wood Service Co.
2727 South Mary Street
Chicago, Illinois 60608

Woodcraft Supply Corp.
313 Montvale Avenue
Woburn, Massachusetts 01801

Cross, Austin and Ireland Lumber Co.
1245 Grand Avenue
Brooklyn, New York

Parker Hardware Co.
27 Ludlow Street
New York, N.Y.

Scheman and Grant Inc (for
Hardware and Tools)
575 Eight Avenue
New York, N.Y.

Atlantic Hardware and Supply Corp.
95 Van Dam Street
New York, N.Y.

Canal Hardware Co., Inc.
311 Canal Street
New York, N.Y.

Black & Decker (tools)
Manufacturing Co.
65–15 Queens Boulevard
Woodside, New York

Introduction

This book has been written for the man or boy who is about to set out on the long road to becoming a woodturner in the true and proper sense of the term. It is hoped that it may smooth out some of the bumps along the way, and so enable him to learn the correct techniques, whilst deriving satisfaction and enjoyment from his hobby. Unfortunately the novice often yields to the strong temptation to do things the apparently easy way, rather than the correct one. However much effort has to be made, it will be worthwhile; for the satisfaction of handling the tools with real skill, sending great streamers of shaving across the workshop, watching the shape appear as if by magic, and achieving a really good finish on the work straight from the cutting tools, must be experienced to be appreciated.

In demonstrating woodturning at exhibitions in many parts of the country, and abroad, I have observed a definite pattern to the queries with which I have to deal. It is largely in response to requests from spectators at such shows, and from correspondents in various parts of the world, that this book has been written, and since I am familiar with the obstacles which loom before the beginner, I hope it may be of value.

There are two distinct methods by which wood can be shaped in a lathe, one of which calls for a considerable amount of skill and manual dexterity, and the other for nothing more than average intelligence. The first, and correct, of these methods involves cutting techniques with proper tools, sharpened as they should be sharpened, and applied correctly to the work. This will leave a near perfect surface, requiring little in the way of abrasive materials. The second method is that of scraping wood to shape, and the man who can be satisfied with it is not in need of this book, or any other. Scraping methods are permissible, but only where it is difficult or dangerous to use cutting methods. This must be appreciated from the very start. The use of scraping tools where cutting tools cannot go is one thing, but the use of scrapers as tools which were designed to cut is indefensible.

The greatest fear among newcomers to turning is that the tools will dig into the whirling wood, and cause an accident. Certainly this can occur if the tools are wrongly shaped, or incorrectly applied to the work, but the beginner must realise that there is no need for it to do so. If the instructions in this book are followed carefully, there will be no danger at all, and progress should be rapid. Unless a thing presents a challenge it is rarely worthwhile, and no challenge will be found in the use of scrapers, except by those who have no real aptitude and are easily pleased.

Scrapers, and scraping techniques, have therefore been dealt with in so far as they are of moment to the true turner, but they must be regarded as a last resort, and never as a quick and easy way to becoming a turner. The making of scrapers from old files, which seems to hold such a fascination for some people, has also been dealt with in passing, but a bench top covered with old files is hardly an indication of a craftsman!

I have deliberately refrained from devoting space to the origins and evolution of the lathe, since this has been done quite often enough already, and can be looked up in the local public library by anyone who happens to be interested. This is not a history book, but it is only fair to say that woodturning as a craft goes a long way back in time, and so the man who can achieve the rank of craftsman on his lathe will have done something very worthwhile. Too many of our country crafts have died already, but it is unlikely that woodturning will go the same way, for which we should be thankful. The machine will do little for you, other than hold the wood in a fixed position, and revolve it at a predetermined speed. The shape is created in your imagination, and arrived at by means of your own skill and dexterity, If, as is my earnest hope, you succeed in mastering the correct techniques with cutting tools, you will have at your fingertips one of the most absorbing and satisfying hobbies in existence. It is not as difficult as many people think. Patience and perseverance will win through in the end, and when things go wrong, as they will on occasions, don't just throw the wood away, find out first just why it happened.

Having had to do all the photographic work my-self, I would like to express my thanks for the advice rendered by Mr John Worthington, and to Mr Brian Cox, for the use of his workshop at a time when I was without one.

Chapter one

The term lathe, for the purposes of this book, refers to woodturning lathes from the small attachments designed to be driven by electric drills, to machines 6ft. or 7ft. (1·8 or 2·1m.) in length, with motors of one to one-and-a-half horsepower. Initial interest in the craft is often aroused by watching professional demonstrators at exhibitions, or in tool stores. This sometimes gives the impression that a big lathe and a wide variety of tools are essential at the start. Nothing could be further from the truth, since very good work indeed can be done on drill driven attachments, using only a few tools. Too many tools can, in fact, be more of a hindrance than a help, unless their true functions and purposes are fully understood.

For the purposes of illustration I have used my own lathe which happens to be a Coronet Major, but modern lathes are very much alike in basic detail. The essential components are the motor unit and drive, headstock, tailstock, bed, saddles, banjos, (tool rest holders), tool rests, driving centre, tailstock centre, and, of course, the feet which hold the bed up clear of the bench.

The heart of the lathe is the headstock, Fig. 1, and the type and quality of the bearing in it can have a great effect on the quality of the work produced. For serious work a really first class adjustable bearing is essential; it has to take heavy end pressure, and must run true at all times, so provision for quick and simple adjustment to take up wear is vital. Any form of lathe where the turning is done directly on the end of the motor spindle should be avoided, except for pure hobby work. On the lathe shown in the photographs it will be noted that there is a really hefty headstock bearing, with an oiler on top of the casting, and that the spindle is carried at the other end in a smaller one.

The headstock bearing itself is, in this case, of tapered phosphor bronze, Fig. 2, adjustment being provided by two castellated rings, which are threaded to the bearing, and can be made to draw it tighter on to the taper of the spindle. With such an arrangement there is no excuse for running with a slack bearing, since this can be rectified in a few minutes. The bearing carrying the other end of the spindle is a roller type, sealed for life, and requiring no attention. Under normal conditions this type of main bearing will run fairly warm, which is quite in order. A point to note here is that these bearings are

Small adjustable woodscrew chuck

Fig. 1

Fig. 2

Fig. 3 (above)

Fig. 4 (below)

keyed internally, and should they ever be dismantled, the key must be correctly replaced.

The lathe shown is the basis of a universal woodworking machine, the left hand end of the spindle being used for mounting circular saws, moulding blocks, and so on, so it has a left hand thread, which is self tightening in use. If the machine is to be used only as a lathe, however, it may be found convenient to mount a grinding wheel at this point. The spindle has an external thread at the right hand, or mandrel end, and an internal number one Morse taper. These, as we shall see, are for the mounting of various accessories.

Since the distance from the driving centre to the bed is $4\frac{1}{2}$in. (112·5mm.), there is a problem in turning large bowls or patterns. This is overcome in an ingenious manner on this particular machine, by splitting the headstock base through the horizontal plane, Fig. 3, and giving a swivelling action by means of a central bolt passing through the bed of the lathe, with a retaining nut, Fig. 4. A small tapered pin is provided for accurate resetting and the lathe can be prepared for large diameter turning in a matter of moments.

Fig. 1 Robust headstock of *Coronet Major* lathe, showing the heavy adjustable bearing on the right, with oiler on top; the three stepped driving pulley, and the nut and washers at the far end of spindle for mounting sawblades, etc.

Fig. 2 Phosphor bronze bearing and its spindle dismantled. Note the keyway on the bearing itself, and the taper on the spindle which fits the internal taper of the bearing

Fig. 3 Close-up showing the way in which the headstock is made so that it can be swung round for the turning of large diameter work. Note the square headed locating pin and also the large nut at the bottom of the picture, which clamps the headstock, in any set position

Fig. 4 How the complete headstock can be swivelled so that the lathe mandrel is at right angles to the bed. Intermediate positions can also be selected

Fig. 5

The power unit is a one horsepower induction unit, totally enclosed, and is mounted on a platform at the rear of the headstock, Fig. 5, in such a manner that it can swing round with the headstock. These motors are brushless and do not interfere with radio or television. Drive is by vee belt, through three stepped pulleys, free running speeds being approximately 1,000, 3,000, and 4,000 revolutions per minute.

The tailstock, Fig. 6, has to be robust and accurately engineered. Like the saddles, it should slide freely on the bed, though with a new machine some stiffness is to be expected. It consists of a main casting containing a poppet barrel, which can be wound in or out by means of a handwheel. The barrel has an internal Morse taper to carry the various centres and attachments, these being self ejecting when the wheel is wound right back. Under the tailstock is a locking lever which enables it to be clamped in any desired position along the bed, and this must always be checked for tightness before starting the machine with work between centres.

Fig. 6

Fig. 7

Fig. 5 Motor mounting on platform. It can be moved backwards or forwards to adjust tension of the belt. The gearbox with its two small controlling levers can be seen quite clearly

Fig. 6 Lathe tailstock, fitted with revolving centre. Note clamping lever on top of the casting to secure the barrel of the tailstock in any desired position, also the large clamping lever at the far side which locks the tailstock itself in position on the lathe bed, and the spring loaded plunger at the bottom of the picture, which allows the complete tailstock to be swung out of the way when necessary

Fig. 7 Lathe saddle in close-up showing the T shaped groove in the upper surface, and the spring-loaded plunger at the bottom of the picture which has a tapered pin engaging in a slot in the lathe bed, locating the saddle in its correct position. The groove can be seen on the left of the picture

11

Fig. 8

Fig. 9

The lathe saddles, Fig. 7, are in effect small sliding platforms, having clamping levers similar to that on the tailstock. There are 'T' sectioned grooves in their upper surfaces to accept the square heads of the bolts which secure the banjos, and the attachments.

The banjos, or tool rest holders, accept the shanks of the tool rests, Fig. 8, and have small clamping levers which will hold these in place at a given height. They are slotted along their length to facilitate the setting of the tool rests in relation to the work. Tool rests themselves have long been the subject of controversy, being made in every shape but the ideal one, Fig. 9. Manufacturers have their heads well in the sand over this, so if you want a good tool rest you will have to follow my example and have some made, but be sure they are strong and rigid. Any vibration set up by these items could affect the work, and if severe could cause an accident.

Most lathes are supplied with a two pronged centre for use at the headstock end, Fig. 11. This will be found suitable for the majority of jobs, but a four-

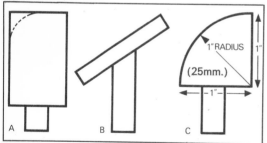

Fig. 10 (above)   Fig. 11 (below)

Fig. 8 Lathe saddle with tool rest holder and tool rest fitted to it. The bolt passing through the tool rest holder has a square head which slides in the T shaped groove of the saddle. Note also the small locking lever which enables the tool rest to be secured at any selected height

Fig. 9 An ideal sectional shape for a tool rest is shown here. It is not, at present, possible to purchase these, but easy to have them made up. It will be seen that wherever the tool is placed on this particular type of rest, the feel of it will be the same

Fig. 10 Sectional shapes of tool rests. A: bad—grind as indicated by dotted line. B: bad. C: ideal shape

Fig. 11 Lathe headstock showing the two pronged driving centre with thread protector and centre extractor, which is a useful item

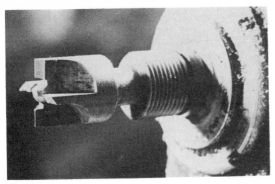

Fig. 12

Fig. 13

pronged version, Fig. 12, is better for slender work or softwoods, where the wedge action of the other type may cause the wood to split under pressure from the tailstock. Manufacturers usually provide a dead centre for the tailstock, Fig. 13, but these are something of an anachronism, and I rarely use one. This type of centre remains stationary while the work spins on it, creating considerable frictional heat, so it is necessary to apply oil or wax to the work, and to adjust the tailstock from time to time to compensate for wear. If this is not done the true centre can be lost and the job ruined, and in an extreme case the wood might even fly from the lathe.

Old books on woodturning often recommend a wooden lathe bed, on the basis that this has an inherent springiness, tending to keep the tailstock centre up to the work, but nowadays one can obtain revolving centres, Fig. 14, which have ball bearings in them, and revolve with the work. When such a centre is used the work can be tightened up fully in the lathe, then slackened slightly to remove some of the pressure, and the tailstock locked. There is then no need for oil or wax, or for

Fig. 14 (above)   Fig. 15 (below)

Fig. 12 A four-pronged driving centre, used on softwoods, and slender work. Note that the central point of this one has become blunted in use, and requires sharpening

Fig. 13 A dead centre fitted to the tailstock. This is a solid piece of metal which remains stationary whilst the wood revolves upon it. It is not, therefore to be recommended

Fig. 14 A revolving centre, which has ball bearings inside it. This type revolves with the work, so requires no lubrication or adjustment during the turning. A worthwhile item, though not cheap

Fig. 15 A cup or ring centre. Note the small spike in the centre. This is a useful item for the turning of wood which is likely to split, and has its uses in the boring of holes through turnings

readjustment during the turning. Cup, or ring centres are also available, Fig. 15, being useful on slender work to prevent splitting. They also have their uses in connection with the drilling of holes through turned work, which I will explain later (see page 73).

The lathe bed should be sturdy and rigid. On the one in the photograph it is a solid steel bar, Fig. 16, having a slot along its full length to take the spring-loaded plungers which are fitted to the tailstock and saddles, so that these can be quickly and easily located. The bed must be kept bright and free from rust at all times, or the sliding of the tailstock and saddles will be impaired. At each end of the bed is a triangular bracket foot, with holes to allow for bolting the machine down to a bench, or to the special cabinet which can be purchased.

Now a word or two on the question of speed in turning. This seems to be a major worry to beginners. The best advice I can give is to use the lowest speed commensurate with bringing off shavings and producing a reasonable surface finish. This will depend to some extent on the type of lathe used, but a speed of roughly 1,000 r.p.m. will be found satisfactory for most purposes as far as turning between centres is concerned. This can be stepped up to about 3,000 r.p.m. for tiny items and for some of the finishing and polishing processes. There is little point in the beginner getting himself bogged down in a mass of theory about all this, since his actual control over the speed of his lathe is normally very limited. Speeds expressed in revolutions per minute can only be relevant in so far as they apply to a given diameter, and the diameter of turned work can vary considerably, quite apart from the fact that it is reducing all the time the tool is cutting. What we are really concerned with is peripheral speed, or the speed of a point on the work expressed in feet per minute. This is virtually impossible to work out on an intricate spindle turning, so I advise you to forget about it. Excessive speed will not help, it overheats the edges of the cutting tools and prevents them from getting a proper bite at the wood; conversely, too little speed will not give a good finish. I began woodturning on a treadle lathe when I was a lad, which is a long time ago, and I suppose a man using such a tool might alter the speed to suit the diameter, but I am sure I never knew what speed I was using at any given time.

Fig. 16 Showing the solid steel lathe bed bar, and the slot which accepts the spring-loaded plungers of saddles and tailstock

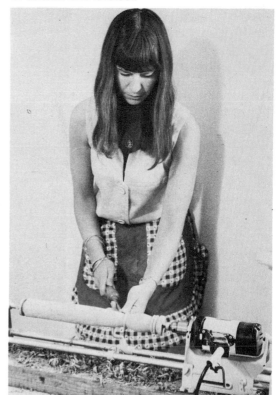

Fig. 17 Lathe attachment and drill in use. These small machines are excellent for anyone wishing to learn the basics of the craft, and also for the turning of small items

On occasions I use a drill-driven lathe attachment, Fig. 17. This has the advantage of a variable speed, controlled by a knurled wheel on the drill. A certain amount of scorn and derision is sometimes directed at tools of this nature, which is a pity, and I often wonder whether the critics have used one, or if indeed they are capable of doing so. I have seen excellent work done with them, and provided their obvious limitations are borne in mind, they are a very good way of getting started in the craft. They are popular with lady turners, and one or two of my pupils have bought them, moving on in time to bigger machines.

The majority of lathes produced today for amateur use will take wood up to about 2ft. 6in. (762mm.) in length between centres, but manufacturers are sometimes asked to supply bed bars 6ft. or 7ft. (1·8 or 2·1m.) in length. There is not much sense in this, since work of that length will whip about all over the place unless the diameter is large, and it is far better to make long articles, such as standard lamps, in two or more sections.

As the purchase of a lathe involves considerable expenditure it is as well to obtain the product of a reputable manufacturer, from whom spares and accessories will be readily available. In addition you will find such firms helpful and sympathetic should you strike any problems with the machine, and the better companies will gladly arrange a demonstration of the tool for you before you buy, so it is worth telephoning the factory concerned to establish this.

Having purchased your lathe it is important to see that it is mounted on a good solid bench which should be bolted to the floor. In some woodturning operations heavy vibration can be set up, and this has to be damped out as far as possible.

The matter of height is important and if possible the lathe should be set up so that its centres are at elbow height to the operator when standing naturally. If the lathe is set lower than this the resultant backache will be most unpleasant.

Lighting must be considered too, and having had to demonstrate woodturning in atrocious lighting conditions on more than one occasion, I am only too well aware of the fact. For general illumination in the workshop strip lighting will do, but the light it gives is very flat and I like to have a movable bulb hanging over the machine if possible.

Chapter two

Certain facts in relation to turning are emphasised in this book, and indeed some are covered more than once. This is quite deliberate and the keen student will do well to pay particular attention to such points and forgive the repetition. One such issue is that of the grinding and shaping of the turning tools. It must be clearly understood at the outset that mastery of the techniques involved in this is a tremendous step towards craftsmanship, and that failure to learn them will effectively prevent the student from achieving complete success, no matter how hard he may try. I am not saying that tool grinding is difficult, it is nothing of the kind, but in many cases too little importance is attached to it—there is an apathetic attitude, which is fatal. No matter how much effort a beginner may put in with badly ground and shaped tools, the result can only be frustration, and possibly danger. This chapter covers what may well be the most important aspect of the craft, so if its contents are absorbed and understood, little difficulty will subsequently be experienced.

I am frequently asked to recommend tutors for woodturning, and it was largely due to this that I started to take pupils myself, but there are not many places one can suggest. Evening classes are very good, as long as it is made quite clear that instruction in cutting techniques is required, rather than scraping.

Going along to watch someone locally who has a lathe may not be a good idea, unless the individual concerned is a woodturner in the true sense of the word. If he is not, bad habits can be acquired, which may be difficult or impossible to eradicate later. Articles and books by authorities on the subject, coupled with plenty of practice, can get the beginner quite a long way, and expert advice is available through woodworking journals, usually by sending in a coupon clipped from the publication, together with your query. These are referred by the editor to specialists in the field, and the process is an excellent means of overcoming the odd stumbling blocks as they occur, particularly since no charge is made for the service. I have numbers of these to answer myself from time to time, and I find them most interesting.

Woodturning is often demonstrated in shops which sell lathes, and here the demonstrator has a critical audience, so he must do things correctly if

Spindle gouge, ground to a nose, being used in a deep hollow he is to show the machine in its best light. Usually he will be pleased to let you examine his tools, and to answer any queries you may have. Remember that if you go anywhere to watch a woodturner, the time will be wasted unless the techniques used are the correct ones. The chap along the road may make some nice table lamps, but it does not follow that his methods are right, or suitable for a beginner to adopt.

It is unfortunate, though understandable, that in many places where woodturning is taught there is a marked reluctance to put gouges and chisels into the hands of the students. I say it is understandable, because great responsibility rests upon the instructor for the safety of his charges, yet it is upon the use of the cutting tools that the beginner is most in need of instruction. As a matter of interest, the only case I know personally where injury was sustained in the course of woodturning, did not involve a cutting tool, but a scraper which was allowed to point upwards instead of down.

Once the selected lathe has been installed in the workshop, some serious thought must be given to the tools and other equipment which will be needed. At this stage I would warn the beginner most strongly against buying anything but the best. The tools and paraphernalia of the turner are by no means expensive, in view of their con- siderable life expectancy, but in any branch of woodturning or woodworking, tools which appear to be cheap probably are—and nasty too! Once you have tried to keep an edge on a piece of cheap steel, and had an opportunity to compare it with the vastly superior qualities of good steel, you will know what I mean. One gets what one pays for, and manufacturers with a good name to protect do not sell poor quality merchandise. A good set of tools, properly ground and cared for, can be a source of pride and it is a pleasure just to handle them. If, as is sometimes the case, the lathe is to be no more than a toy, to be played with once in a while, a few cheap tools and some self-tuition may suffice. If, on the other hand, the aim is to master the true craft of woodturning and to achieve a professional finish the selection of a really good set of tools, and the careful preparation of them for use, is a truly vital matter.

There is frequently a tendency in the early stages to gather together far too many tools. A vast array

Fig. 1 A useful set of tools for the beginner. Two skews, a parting tool, two gouges for spindle work, a bowl gouge, roughing gouge, and a round-nosed scraper

of shining chisels and gouges looks good, I agree, but this can lead to utter confusion just as a bag brimming with clubs would confuse a novice golfer. Seven or eight tools are enough to begin with, and when these can be used with skill and confidence, others can be added. Advice about turning tools is hard to come by, and shops which keep a good selection are rare. Of those who do stock tools, most keep only boxed sets, and although some of these are quite good, there are some which omit important items, and include unnecessary ones. If difficulty is experienced on this point, which is very likely, a letter to a good tool manufacturer will usually bring a catalogue and price list. From this, tools can be ordered by post, with or without handles, which the turner normally makes for himself.

When a drill-driven lathe attachment is used, the tools designed for it should be employed, since these are small and will not overload the drill motor. Do not use these small tools on big machines, for which they are not intended, or an accident may result. As a guide to the beginner, a basic set of tools is shown in Fig. 1, and is made up of the following:

$\frac{1}{4}$in. (6·4mm.) spindle gouge
$\frac{3}{4}$in. (19·1mm.) half round roughing gouge
$\frac{1}{2}$in. (12·7mm.) skew chisel
$1\frac{1}{2}$in. (37·5mm.) skew chisel
Parting tool
Round-nosed scraper
$\frac{3}{8}$in. (9·5mm.) deep long and strong gouge
Shallow $\frac{1}{2}$in. (12·7mm.) spindle gouge

It is not always appreciated that new woodturning tools usually have to be ground to the correct shape by the turner before they can be used, and unless this is done a good deal of trouble will be experienced. This is fairly general, although one or two enlightened firms are beginning to provide ready ground tools. Woodturning tools have one continuous bevel each side in the case of chisels, and one continuous bevel on the outside in the case of scrapers, but they do not under any circumstances have a second bevel, as is the case with normal woodworking tools, and this fact is vitally important.

The novice should stamp indelibly on his mind the one fact which will help him most to achieve success with safety in his turning. This is that, with the single exception of scraping tools, the bevel must rub the work all the time the tool is cutting. If the bevel rubs correctly, the tool will not dig into the wood, whereas if the tool is applied to the work without the bevel rubbing there is every chance that it will dig into the wood—it is as simple as that. I will come back to this matter of digging in later, but it is this more than anything else, that puts beginners off, and fear of it can prevent them from building up the confidence they need. It can be dangerous, and at best is disconcerting, but if the tools are shaped as they should be, and applied correctly to the work, it will not happen. If a skilled man has a dig with a cutting tool it is the result of nonchalance, carelessness, or inattention, and as the skill of the student grows he will find that he is dealing with incipient digs and snatches by instinct, just as a skilled car driver corrects a skid.

The sketches which indicate how the bevels should be ground need to be studied carefully, Figs 2 and 3, because it is pointless to make any attempt to use the tools until they are absolutely as they ought to be. It will be noted that the bevel must be either a dead straight line from heel to edge, as is the case when grinding has been done on the side of the wheel, or a concave shape, as when the edge of the wheel has been used. The practice of grinding on the side of the wheel is not recommended, since the frictional heat produced is considerable, with a chance of drawing the temper of the metal. If this occurs, the preservation of a keen cutting edge for more than a few minutes will be rendered impossible. It has been said that a tool which is hollow ground from the edge of the wheel

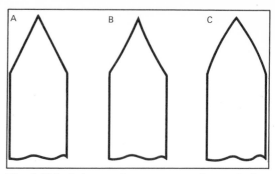

Fig. 2 Chisel shapes. A: correct—as from grinding on side of wheel. B: correct—as from grinding on edge of wheel. C: incorrect—shaped in this way the tool will dig in

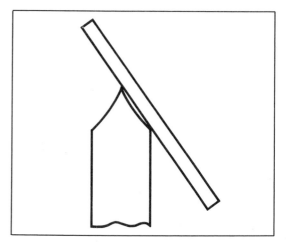

Fig. 3 Exaggerated view of oilstone bridging the gap on tool which has been hollow ground

is more likely to dig in, but I do not accept this, having ground my tools so for years. With a bevel which is concave the oilstone bridges across it, so there is less metal to be removed, and less likelihood of rounding over the extreme edge, which must be avoided at all costs.

I would like, if I can, to clear up one of the real red herrings which crosses the trail of the student turner, this being the question of the exact angle which should be measured and ground on the cutting tools. This in fact will vary according to the

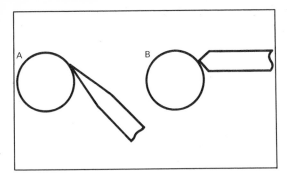

Fig. 4 How angle ground on tool affects the position of the handle. A: long bevel—handle low. B: short bevel—handle high

Fig. 5 Two small oilstone slips, which are most useful. One is kept for gouges and scrapers, the other for chisels

height of the turner himself, and that of his lathe, and I have no idea what the angle is on any of my tools. There is far too much attention paid to all this, and my advice is to put away the protractor, and look at the matter in a different light. Let me repeat what I said earlier—the bevel must rub the work all the time the tool is cutting. That is unless, like some I have seen, you are using all the tools in the box as scrapers! It follows, therefore, that the angle ground on the tool simply dictates the position in which the handle will lie if the bevel rubs as it should. The sketch Fig. 4 will show what I mean fairly well. Assuming correct use of the tool, too long a bevel will mean holding the handle too low for comfort, and too short a bevel will mean holding it too high. It is precisely for this reason that no professional turner will use tools other than his own if it can be avoided. I have had to do so on odd occasions, and there has usually been nothing wrong with the tools, but the feel has not been right. Extending this a little, you will see that a short man with a lathe mounted high would need long bevels, whereas a tall man whose lathe was mounted low would need short ones.

Tools which have been correctly ground can be used without further treatment on coarse grained woods such as elm and oak, but will require honing on an oilstone for most timbers, and for really fine work a leather strop may have to be employed. Amateurs in woodwork often make the grave mistake of continuing to use a tool long after its edge has become dull, looking upon sharpening as a waste of time, which it certainly is not. There

is nothing quite like the feel of a really sharp tool working, and nothing worse than gnawing away at a piece of wood with a blunt one. Big oilstones, of the type used by woodworkers, are not really suitable for turning tools, although they can be used. Small oilstone slips are much handier, the grades used being medium and fine, Fig. 5. The reason for this is that turning tools are honed by rubbing the stone on the tool, rather than the other way about, and if this method is adopted from the start there is less danger of the edge being rounded over. A minimum of two of these slips will be needed, one being kept exclusively for gouges, and the other for chisels. The gouges will wear hollows in a slip in a very short time, thus rendering it useless for sharpening a chisel.

The accepted way of honing tools is shown in Fig. 6, the tool being firmly supported on some convenient object, and held stationary while the stone is moved·on it with a circular motion. This is a little art in itself, if the fatal rounding over of the edge is to be avoided, but it is easily and rapidly learned. It is by no means unusual for sets of turning tools to be brought to me to be ground, and I oblige when I can, but I fear that in many cases the owner takes them away and relies solely upon the oilstone to keep them sharp, with the inevitable result that the edges are gradually rounded over, and the tools become increasingly hard to control. The sketch (Fig. 7) will clarify this. What actually happens is easy enough to understand, and it goes back to our golden rule which says the bevel must rub the work. With a bevel shaped as it should be, there is

19

Fig. 6
Fig. 7

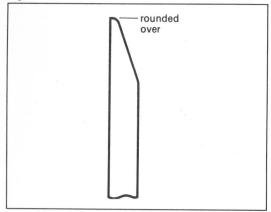

rounded
over

Fig. 6 Sharpening a round-nosed scraper with a coarse oilstone. The tool is rested on a convenient object, and the stone is moved with a circular motion, working around the edge of the tool. The wire edge is left on

Fig. 7 Effect of bad oilstoning on a gouge. The extreme edge has become dubbed and the handle must be lifted to get the edge to cut. This removes the support of the bevel and the tool will dig in

no difficulty, but once the edge is rounded it is necessary to lift the tool handle to get the edge in contact with the work, thus removing the support of the bevel, and so the tool digs in. By rounding over the edge, we have created what is, in effect, a second bevel, which just will not do!

Bear in mind that the function of the grindstone is to shape the tools, and that of the oilstone to trim up the rough edge and impart that final touch of sharpness. If your tools are to be a credit to you the two must work as a team.

On the subject of grindstones, it is often said that turning tools must not be sharpened on a dry wheel, only on a wet one. This advice is frequently given on labels attached to new tools, and is sound advice too, but hardly practical for most of us. Wet stones are large, ponderous, expensive things, not often found in the home workshop, so we have to manage as best we can with a carborundum wheel. I have been using one for years, and my tools seem happy enough, but grinding must be done with care, or good steel will be ruined. When a grinding machine is to be used, some sort of protection must be given to the eyes, which could be injured by flying particles of steel or carborundum. A good pair of goggles, Fig. 8, will do, or a face visor. Never take any chances in this matter, your eyes are far too precious. A pot of water is kept handy and the tools are dipped into it from time to time to dissipate the frictional heat generated on the wheel. Very little pressure is applied, and the job cannot be hurried. The tool rests on the wheel under little more than its own weight. If too much pressure is applied, the tool will overheat quickly, especially in the case of the smaller tools which have less metal to carry away the heat.

Let us consider the grinding of a basic kit of tools, and look at the shapes they need in order to fulfil their appointed duties. The spindle gouges are ground to a nose, so that they can be used down in hollows, and in Fig. 9 and 10, you can see one of these being ground. It is held firmly, as still as possible in relation to the wheel, and slowly rolled from side to side so that all the surface is ground. An even bevel all round is what is wanted, and this is a little difficult for the beginner, but practice makes perfect. Grinding commences on the heel of the bevel, and the tool is tipped slowly forward until it is in the right position. My own

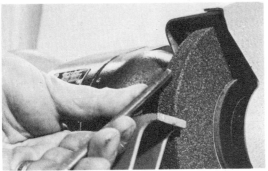

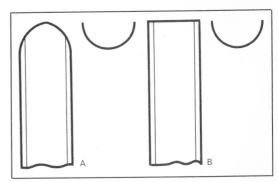

Fig. 9 (above)　　　　Fig. 8 (below)　　Fig. 10 (above)　　　　　　Fig. 11 (below)

Fig. 8 A good strong pair of goggles should always be worn when the grinder is used, and a face mask, like the one shown, is vital for sanding operations

Fig. 9 Here a small spindle gouge is being ground. Hold the tool steady and roll it slowly from side to side with light pressure

Fig. 10 Shapes of gouges. A: spindle gouges are ground to a nose. B: roughing gouges are ground straight across

Fig. 11 Grinding a roughing gouge, the bevel being kept fairly steep, and you can see that the end of the tool is ground straight across

tools are ground right up to the edge, and I can tell when this has been reached by the sparks which begin to come over the top of the blade. This is the point at which the steel is most likely to be burned, so the water pot must be used, and great care taken. Some turners prefer to grind almost to the edge and finish off on the oilstone, but it is a matter of choice, and the end result is the same.

The $\frac{3}{4}$in. (19·1mm.) half round roughing gouge is not ground to a nose, but straight across, Fig. 11, because it will be used for roughing down from the square and for general shaping. There is no need to worry about the corners catching in the work, although they certainly look as though they might, in practice they do not, at least not if the tool is used properly. The bevel on these roughing gouges is kept fairly steep, or short, probably somewhere around 45 degrees. It is rolled from side to side in

21

Fig. 12

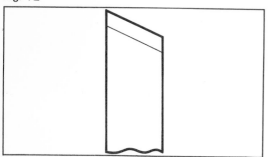

Fig. 13 (above)   Fig. 14 (below)

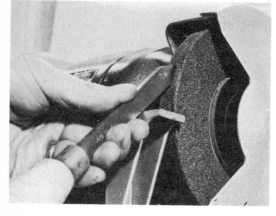

Fig. 12 A skew chisel. The reason for its name is quite obvious from this photograph, the end of the blade being ground at an angle rather than square

Fig. 13 Shape of a skew chisel

Fig. 14 Grinding a parting tool. Note that the angle at the end of this tool should never be allowed to become too obtuse

the grinding, as with the spindle gouges, aiming for an even bevel all round. This tool grinding may sound difficult, but it will come with practice, and until it has been mastered all sorts of problems are likely to arise when the tools are in use.

The ends of the skew chisels are not ground straight across, but at an angle to the blade, Fig. 12 and 13, hence the name. They are one of the easiest tools to grind, being moved slowly from side to side on the wheel. The bevel should be the same width on each side of the tool, since the turner has to be ambidextrous, and the chisel will be used in both directions along the work. If the bevels are unequal, the feel will be wrong.

The shape of the parting tool is quite critical, a point which is not always appreciated, and the photographs and sketches showing this should be studied carefully, Fig. 14 and 15. The bevel angle should be fairly acute, and there is an unfortunate tendency to allow this to become progressively more obtuse with successive grindings, causing the tool to kick back in use, which is rather alarming. As viewed from above in its cutting position, the blade is ground in, or relieved, behind the cutting edge, so that it will not bind when taken deep into the work.

The round-nosed scraper is a different kettle of fish altogether. It is not a cutting tool in the true sense of the word, being used in a position of negative rake, with the handle end higher than the blade edge. If a tool is to be used thus, it is immediately obvious that the bevel cannot rub the work, and is therefore relatively unimportant. It should be noted, however, that if the bevel is too long there will be insufficient metal to support the edge, or to carry away the frictional heat, as the sketch Fig. 16 shows. Scrapers can be used after a quick rub round on the grindstone, leaving the wire edge which is formed in the process, and this is my own preference when I use them, which is not too often. They have their uses in faceplate work, but should be reserved for cuts which are difficult or unsafe for a gouge. Little skill is needed to scrape wood about, and the finish from scrapers is poor, especially if they are pushed hard into the wood. On spindle work they should not be used at all. Note that these tools must not be pointed upwards in use, the sketch Fig. 17 illustrates the point, and you will see that if the tool is properly used the wood can only knock it away, whereas if it is pointed upwards it can be wrenched into the work with unpleasant results.

Scrapers can be sharpened on a coarse oilstone, using a circular motion, and leaving a wire edge which will cut quite well. Never remove the wire edge from a scraper, since it is this alone which cuts. Another method is to stone the edge, remove the wire that is formed, and turn the edge over as a cabinet maker sharpens his scraper. I do not like this method, because the edge soon fades.

New oilstone slips soak up oil at a phenomenal rate, so they should be left to soak overnight in a tin. I

Fig. 15 Parting tool shape. A: shape of tool face. B: shape of edge. Tool is ground in to prevent binding

Fig. 16 Side view of scrapers. A: angle too shallow. There is not enough metal to hold an edge and the tool will overheat. B: a better angle

Fig. 17 A: a scraper pointed up like this can be wrenched into the work and cause an accident. B: a scraper inclined down can only be pushed away by the revolving wood. No danger is involved

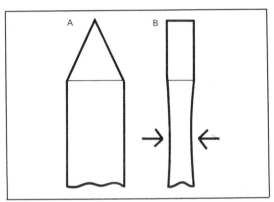

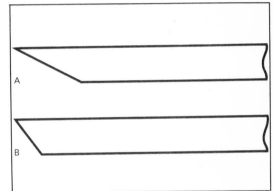

Fig. 15 (above)   Fig. 17A (below)   Fig. 16 (above)   Fig. 17B (below)

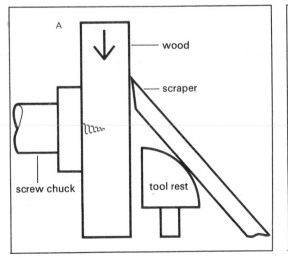

use a mixture of one part thin oil to one of paraffin on mine, and find it excellent, but it is important to use the stone correctly, or all the care which has gone into the grinding will be to no avail. Taking the $\frac{3}{4}$in. (19·1mm.) half round roughing gouge as an example, the first requirement is a suitable spot in the workshop which is the right height to support the tool while it is honed. If your handles are long, as they should be, you can steady them against your leg, which is a help. Fig. 18 shows the action. Some oil is put on the stone, and with the gouge comfortably settled, operations are begun on the heel of the bevel, using a circular motion, and bringing the stone slowly over until it is cutting right across the bevel. The correct position will be shown when oil begins to creep over the cutting edge. If this position of stone relative to blade can be maintained, and the gouge rolled slowly back and forth during the stoning, a fine edge will be produced with a few moments' work. The temptation to bring the stone too far over, just to make sure, must be resisted, for if the tool is to behave as it should, there must be no dubbing of the edge whatsoever. A wire edge will be left inside the gouge, and this can be removed with a few light strokes of the stone towards the edge, but in practice the wood will knock it off anyway.

It is sometimes possible to fit a grindstone on the other side of the headstock, in fact when I have a long run of turning I fit one where the sawblade usually goes. This is convenient, because it means that a tool can be trued up in a few seconds without moving from the lathe, but the speed of the machine must be kept low, or the stone may disintegrate, especially if it has received a knock at some time. It is better to have an independent grinder in the workshop, but beware of the small cheap versions, which revolve too fast, and may burn the tools. There is a mistaken impression among amateurs that no damage has been done until the metal turns blue, but this is not so, the temper can be drawn long before that happens.

Overheating of the turning tools, and consequent loss of temper, can be due to bad grinding, but it also occurs when a tool is blunt, or incorrectly applied to the work, so that it rubs without cutting. Beginners in bowl turning often fall foul of this, even to the extent of raising smoke from the job and burning the work, yet the answer is simple enough. The tools must be kept really sharp all the

time, and the minute they cease to bring off a shaving the turning must stop until the reason has been established. Time is not wasted in sharpening tools, but a great deal is wasted in trying to use blunt ones.

The stoning of other gouges is done in exactly the same way and the parting tool and chisels present no problems, though there is obviously no need to roll the tool.

Turning tools are sold in two varieties, these being normal, and what are known as long and strong. The beginner is advised to leave the latter alone until they become necessary, because they are far more difficult for him to grind and sharpen than the standard versions, and their thick blades do not give the feel of what is happening—thinner blades are far more sensitive.

As I mentioned earlier, a gouge or chisel can be used on some woods straight from the grindstone, but we should now consider exactly what the object is. The whole aim of sharpening efforts is to get the best possible finish on the wood straight from the cutting edge, with as little need for abrasive materials as possible. This is where experience and skill come in, and if you watch a professional you will see that he uses very little abrasive paper, except in certain special cases. The grades he uses are medium down to flour, coarser stuff will leave rings round the work, and defeat the object. In trying to get this excellent finish from the cutting tools, you do not have to be unduly fussy in the roughing out stages, but towards the end the thing becomes more critical. The last few cuts must be taken lightly, with razor sharp tools which have come fresh from the oilstone. Those who have watched me at exhibitions may have noticed that I stop and sharpen the tools for these final cuts, and I never grudge the time it takes, because time is in fact saved by this process. If you leave a bad finish from the tools and try to sand it away, you will find that this is a messy and difficult business; one light cut with a sharp gouge or chisel will do what would take minutes with abrasives.

Because of this, the purist will have special fine stones for these occasions, and may even follow up with leather-covered stropping boards made to fit the individual tools. These are worth having,

Fig. 18 Honing a gouge with the oilstone. The tool must be firmly supported, and if the handle can be steadied against the body so much the better. Use a circular motion of the stone, rolling the tool at the same time

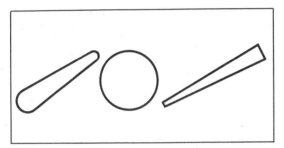

Fig. 19 Some sectional shapes of stropping boards which are covered in soft leather

Fig. 20 Large tools are sometimes very useful for the rapid removal of wood on large jobs. This photograph shows two large gouges, one shallow and one half round, also a 2in. [50·8mm.] skew chisel

though I only use them when the timber is awkward, and they must be kept in a box, away from dust and grit. Any wood will do, shaped as required, and covered with soft leather into which fine emery paste has been rubbed. In use these boards are drawn towards the edge from the handle end, if you do it the other way they will not last very long! Some typical shapes are shown in the sketch, Fig. 19, and for the small tools a piece of leather rolled or folded to fit will do. Remember that this ultra fine edge is only for the final cuts, in practice it will not last very long.

The full uses of all the turning tools will be seen as we go along, but now let us look at some of the other equipment which will be needed. A study of a manufacturer's catalogue will reveal a tremendous range of tools, but this need not alarm the beginner, for he is unlikely to need them all, and certainly not for a long time to come. I am often asked why I carry so many tools with me as I travel round, and the reason is that many of them are duplicated, so that a good session on the grindstone will keep me going for some time. Gouges, in the main, are for the rapid removal of wood, and in roughing down the larger the work the larger the gouge used. There is a limit to this, however, determined by the power available, since a really big gouge can put too much strain on a small motor. I have two big ones which I find most useful, Fig. 20, these being a shallow 2in. (50·8mm.), and a half round one and a $\frac{1}{4}$in. (6·4mm.). These I use on big lamps, wine table centre pillars, table legs, and so on. Tools like this can considerably reduce the time taken to rough out the work, but I do not recommend their use until the small ones can be handled really well.

It seems to me that one of the first things the newcomer to woodturning wants to do is to make scraping tools out of old files, which is a harmless enough pastime, but not really worth the bother. There is a case for it in making up some tool for a special job, where no standard tool is suitable, but after all the careful grinding is done, the things still look remarkably like old files, and rather out of place on a craftsman's bench. Only about two scrapers are really needed, and they are cheap enough in all conscience, so I suppose it is just that some people like to say that they make their own tools. Should anyone wish to indulge in the practice, it is simple enough as the sketch Fig. 21

shows. The outer casing of the file on its upper surface is ground away to get at the softer metal underneath, and some sort of bevel is put on. The actual shape of the thing is a matter of personal taste.

The lending of tools is never a good idea, at least in my experience, and this applies strongly in the case of turning chisels and gouges. Getting these tools ground up so that they feel right can take quite a time, and a very little of someone else's use and sharpening can undo all the good work.

Do not be disheartened if in the early days some-one walks into the workshop and says all your carefully ground angles are too long or too short. It is almost inevitable, and it happens to me at exhibitions, but I have learned to live with it! The tools are ground to suit the user, and no one else, and as long as they do so, all is well.

Turners love to argue about the length and shape of tool handles. It is a waste of time. What is needed is a functional handle which suits the user and feels comfortable. Handles for use on big lathes should be long enough to be steadied against the body when necessary—and it often is on big work if you are in a hurry and want to take heavy cuts. Another point in relation to handles concerns the dreaded dig-in, which is such a worry in the early days. If the tool has a decent handle, which is firmly held, a dig will do little more than damage the work, or cause the drive belt to slip. If, on the other hand, the handle is inadequate, or the tool loosely held, there is every chance of an accident. Concentrate all the time on keeping the bevel rubbing the wood, and producing shavings rather than dust, and the problem of the dig-in will, like the proverbial old soldier, slowly fade away. Any sort of hardwood will really do for tool handles, but obviously it should not be short grained, and you may find it a good idea to vary the woods used, to facilitate recognition of the various tools among the shavings and general debris.

Looking after turning tools is really more a matter of common sense than anything, the main enemy being rust, which can be dealt with in a number of ways. If you leave plenty of shavings around these will absorb moisture from the air, and it is a good excuse for not clearing up. I regret to say that I do not have a tidy mind, as those who have

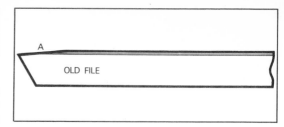

Fig. 21 Making a scraping tool from an old file. Grind away surface at A to reveal the softer metal and shape end as required

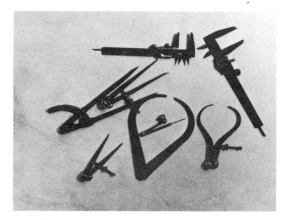

Fig. 22 A selection of useful dividers and calipers for measuring work in connection with turning

visited my workshop will appreciate, but for those who do, a good tool rack, preferably on castors, is a good idea, and a rub with an oily rag will keep the blades bright.

This applies also to the bright parts of the lathe, where I regard even the most minute speck of rust with the emotions of a gardener examining a grub on his prize rose! If you keep your tools in drawers or boxes, you will find anti-rust paper, as sold by good tool shops, a great asset. Laid in the bottom of the box, it will work like a charm. Some people with real moisture problems have little bags of silica gel around, which helps too. A portable tool rack is a good thing, especially if made so that it can revolve, but don't build a lot of little trays and divisions into it to hold the small tools. These will only fill up with shavings which streak from your lathe, and cleaning them out is not funny.

Some woodturning operations set up quite a lot of vibration, and if you fall into my bad habit of keeping the tools and general effects on the bench, you will have to clear the decks for these jobs, or valuable small items will be shaken on to the floor, and shovelled up with the rubbish.

There are some other tools which I will briefly mention here and full details of their uses will be dealt with later. Some sort of bradawl is a must, and you can have the normal carpenter's type, or the birdcage maker's awl, which has a square sectioned blade. I prefer this, and you could make one for yourself easily enough. This tool was originally designed for making holes through thin wood near the edges without splitting it, but we will be using it mainly for marking the centres of square work, and making lead holes for faceplate and woodscrew chuck screws.

Fig. 22 shows some of these tools, dividers and calipers being very important, and it is difficult to have too many of these if you are intending to do much repetition work.

Chapter three

When the lathe and turning tools have been obtained, and the latter ground and sharpened correctly, we can begin to think about starting some woodturning, but there are one or two matters which merit discussion first.

High on the list comes the perennial question — which are the best woods for turning? I have a sneaking suspicion that people who ask me this really mean what are the easiest woods to turn, which is not the same thing. There is in any case no short answer to the problem, one can give an opinion and that is all. The turner will soon have his own favourites, and in my case yew, elm, and sycamore would be well in front. It must be realised that not only do different species have varying characteristics, but there can be great differences in pieces of wood of the same species, once they are in the lathe. I have only encountered one piece of wood with which I was unable to do anything, and that was a piece of Jarra, which is full of minerals, and produces a shower of sparks from the tools. It is like trying to turn a piece of stone. Other woods, such as teak and elm will take the edges off the tools quickly, but not to such a marked degree. Timber with a fairly high moisture content is more satisfying and spectacular to turn than dry stuff, but likely to shrink and split after it is turned. Grain must be considered too, for often it is the piece of wood with difficult, or even really nasty grain formation which gives the best appearance after turning, if the turner has the skill to cope with it. Some timbers are obnoxious to the nose, causing sneezing and sinus irritation, and others can bring out sensitive skins in a rash. The best advice for a beginner is to try any piece of wood he can lay his hands on, and form his own opinions, but he should not blame the wood if the finish is poor. This is probably not where the fault lies, and each piece of wood will be a challenge to him. Good timber is expensive, and difficult to obtain, so one cannot be fussy.

The following list of some of the better known woods is not intended to be complete, but it may help someone who is just starting, the comments being drawn purely from my own experience.

Table lamp turned in yew and polished by burnishing with its own shavings

Oak: Open grain, coarse, not too interesting except when figured. Very hard, and not recommended for beginners, especially in bowl work.

Ash: Hard, pleasing grain, pale colour and good texture. Turning characteristics are good and articles made in it sell well.

Elm: Varies a lot. Dulls tools quickly, but has rich colour and interesting grain. It can look very good when a few knots are present, but it is not too stable and should be polished immediately after being turned.

Sycamore: Turns easily, and has good finishing qualities. Used a good deal in laminated work because of its light colour, but apt to be hard to obtain.

Chestnut: Similar to oak, pleasant to turn but not easy to get.

Lime: The carver's timber, much like sycamore in appearance, but very soft.

Walnut: Expensive, but worth buying for special jobs. Striking dark colour and grain is interesting. Turns well.

African Walnut: Turns very easily, being quite soft. Honey coloured, often with distinctive black lines.

Yew: Excellent if you can get it in suitable sizes. Turns like soap, and will come to a high gloss from friction with its own shavings. A really beautiful timber to work.

Beech: Not much to look at, but easy to obtain and relatively cheap.

Rosewood: Dark brown to purple in colour. Oily. Turns well but very expensive indeed.

Teak: Easy to turn, oily, hard on tool edges, and expensive. Useful as a dark timber in laminated work, but its poor glueing qualities should be remembered.

Maple: Uninteresting, but easy to turn and has a pleasant texture.

Holly: Hard to get in a seasoned condition, very light in colour and hard. Good for laminated work.

I could go on, but this will be enough to get the beginner under way.

Another question which is always cropping up concerns obtaining supplies of timber suitable for turning. There are firms and individuals who will supply timber selected for the purpose, and although this can appear a little expensive, one must remember that the supplier has to stand the wastage problem; what you receive is sound timber. Such firms advertise in the woodworking press, and will deliver in reasonable quantities almost anywhere. As an alternative, why not go along to a good class joinery firm and have a chat with the yard foreman? Offcuts to him are often small baulks of timber to us, and they can be bought quite cheaply. An added advantage is that only good quality well-seasoned wood is used in such places.

As a matter of interest, I once bought a pile of old fence posts from a farmer, intending to burn them. They were round posts with the bark still on, and although they had rotted where they had been in the ground, there was still a lot of good wood in them, and they produced a large number of table lamps at very little cost. All kinds of wood were among them, but if you try a source such as this, watch out for nails and staples. As far as home-grown timbers go, a run round some of the small country sawmills can be fruitful, but try to go on a weekday when they are not too busy. You will often find quite good stuff lying around in the plank. This can look cheap, but there is almost certain to be waste.

So, obtaining wood is one thing, preparing it for turning is another. It is useful to have a store of blanks ready for use, or you can keep the wood in the plank, cutting it up as you need it. If you cut it up, and intend to store it, I would recommend that the ends of squares and the edges of discs be coated liberally with old paint, or wax, which will inhibit the drying process. If this is not done you may have a nasty shock when you examine your hoard and find that it has split badly.

In the case of a block which is to be turned between centres, lines are drawn at the ends, from corner to corner, to locate the centre, and a bradawl is pushed in at the intersections, to facilitate mounting the block in the lathe. The other marking method shown in Fig. 1 will do if you prefer it. The blocks can be sawn or planed to an octagonal shape, and for the real beginner this is a good idea, but the centres should be marked first, Fig. 2. Professional turners do not bother with this, since

Fig. 1 (above)

Fig. 2 (below)

Fig. 3

for them it is quicker and easier to take off the corners with a gouge, but in the early stages the idea of attacking a whirling square of wood with a cutting tool may be a little off-putting, and the removal of the corners first may help to build confidence. In school workshops when pupils are using the lathe the corners are certainly best removed, and anyway they make excellent kindling wood.

If the wood is mounted in the lathe with care, there should be no problems, but the procedure must be followed correctly. I have never had a piece of wood fly from a lathe, but it can happen, and there are those with scars to prove it. The driving centre is fitted to the mandrel together with the centre ejector, if any, Fig. 3. If you have a revolving centre, this can be fitted to the tailstock, but if not you can use the dead centre provided, applying some lubricant to the wood first. The poppet barrel should be wound back into the tailstock first, since running with undue projection here causes unnecessary strain.

Fig. 1 Method of marking the ends of squares to locate the centre, as an alternative to the usual process of drawing in the diagonals

Fig. 2 When the centres of a square have been accurately marked, the corners can be removed on a sawbench or, as in this case, on a small planer. This is not absolutely necessary

Fig. 3 Centres which become jammed in the internal taper of the mandrel can be removed quite easily if the centre ejector is fitted. Here a steel bar is being used to shift a stubborn centre

Now the block is placed against the driving centre, the point of which goes into the bradawl mark, and the tailstock is slid along so that its centre engages with the wood in like manner, Fig. 4. Lock the tailstock firmly with its clamping lever so that it cannot move on the bed, then wind the centre forward by means of the handwheel until the fangs

Fig. 4

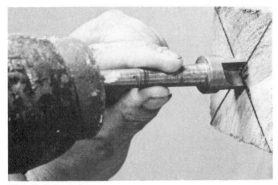

Fig. 5 (above)

Fig. 6 (below)

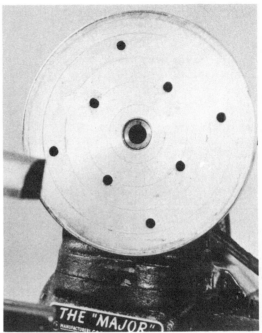

Fig. 7

Fig. 4 A square of wood with centres marked at each end and a bradawl hole made has been fitted in the lathe. The bradawl marks help in engaging driving and tailstock centres

Fig. 5 On hardwoods the driving centre can be tapped in with a copper or hide mallet, as shown

Fig. 6 Using a saw to make a slot so that the driving centre can be engaged without undue pressure on the lathe bearing

Fig. 7 Faceplate fitted to the lathe mandrel. Note the two sets of holes through which screws are passed to hold the work

of the driving centre are buried in the wood. Turn the tailstock handwheel back half a turn to relieve the strain, and lock it. This is the method on wood which is soft, but if the wood is hard the driving centre should be driven into it first with a copper mallet, Fig. 5, or a sawcut made to take the centre, Fig. 6. This is to avoid undue strain on the lathe bearings. At this point the tool rest would be put

in position, but we will come to that on page 34.

For the moment, let us consider the mounting of faceplate work. Bowls, platters, egg cups, ashtrays, and the like will not have the benefit of tailstock support; in fact a fair description of faceplate work is any job which is supported only at the headstock end, the term embracing work which is held in various forms of chuck, apart from the faceplate itself. On bowls or discs more than about 8in. (203mm.) in diameter, the faceplate will be used, Fig. 7. This screws on to the mandrel, and is self tightening in use. With new machines, faceplates can sometimes jam, especially if left on the machine overnight. This is because they pick up heat from the bearing during the turning, and so expand and tighten a little more on to the mandrel. When allowed to cool, they will obviously contract, and so jam tight. The trouble can be cured by placing a fibre washer behind the plate, but if you get one really stuck, it may be necessary to screw a batten to it, and strike this sharply (in the right direction), Fig. 8. This will certainly shift it, and is preferable to some of the more brutal methods I have seen used.

The faceplate is provided with a number of holes, in this case eight, and the work is attached to it with screws. Short, fat screws should be used, and don't forget them when you are turning, or the work may be spoiled, together with the tool in use. If you have a bandsaw, the square for a bowl or dish will be cut to a circle before turning, but if not the wood can be brought to an octagonal shape by hand, or on the sawbench, Fig. 9.

A very useful alternative to the faceplate is the woodscrew chuck, Fig. 10, which comes in two sizes. The 1½in. (37·5mm.) version relies entirely upon a single central screw to hold the wood, but the 2½in. (62·5mm.) one has holes for two additional screws. Ordinary No. 14 steel counter-sunk screws are used. They can easily be replaced if damaged, and can also be adjusted for protection from the face, which is useful. For small items such as egg cups, knobs, and such like, the smaller chuck is used, Fig. 11, so that its base does not get in the way of the cutting tools. The bigger one will take work up to 8in. or 9in. (203mm. or 228·5mm.) in diameter.

Beginners tend to be sceptical about the holding powers of these chucks, especially the smaller one, expecting the work to fly off at any moment. In my experience, this is most unlikely to happen if the wood is put on properly in the first place, unless too much pressure is used, or there is a dig-in. Small blocks on the single screw should not be more than about 3in. (75mm.) in length, and all will be well. If the work has to be longer than this,

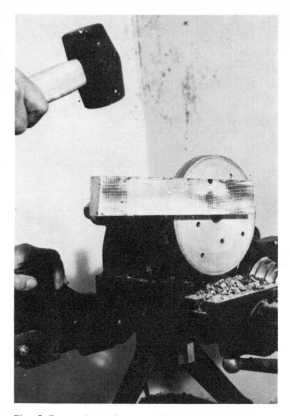

Fig. 8 Removing a jammed faceplate by striking a batten which has been screwed to it

as when turning vases, the larger chuck should be used, or some tailstock support should be given until the work is roughed out.

Removal of these chucks from the mandrel presents no problems, since there is a hole in the chuck to take a tommy bar, and a sharp tap always does the trick, Fig. 12. There are other ways of mounting faceplate work for special jobs, and we will deal with these as we come to them. Correct tensioning of the driving belt seems to bother some beginners, and I would say that the belt should be tight enough not to slip when heavy cuts are made, but not so tight as to strain the motor bearing. About ½in. (12·7mm.) movement in the centre will do. Tensioning of the belt is done by moving the motor back or forward on its mounting.

Fig. 9 (above)

Fig. 10 (above)

Fig. 11 (below)

Whilst I would certainly not say that woodturning is dangerous, accidents do sometimes happen, and it is not a bad idea to fit the starter switch in such a position that it can be knocked 'off' with the knee, should the occasion ever arise. Safety with lathes is a matter of common sense, but there are people with very little. Sleeves should always be rolled up, ties should not be worn, nor loose floppy clothing. Tools must contact the tool rest before they touch the work, and one should never lean over the lathe while it is running.

Many of the illustrations in this book could, and probably will, be criticised because the machine is shown without guards. These have been taken off for clarity, but they should *always* be used. All the photographs were taken with the machinery switched off, so there was no danger.

Fig. 9 If no bandsaw is available, discs for bowl work can be brought to octagonal shape on the sawbench

Fig. 10 Two sizes of woodscrew chuck as available for the Coronet machine. On the left is the 2½in. [63·3mm.] version, with holes for two extra screws. On the right is the 1½in. [37mm.] chuck with a single central screw

Fig. 11 (below left) A 1½in. [37mm.] woodscrew chuck shown stripped down. The small pronged instrument is used to tighten up the central threaded portion thus holding the screw firmly

Fig. 12 (below) Removing a jammed woodscrew chuck by means of a steel bar and a sharp tap from a piece of wood

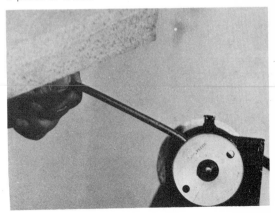

Chapter four

Spindle turning is an expression used to describe operations in which the work is supported at both ends, between centres, rather than at one end only, as in faceplate work. The beginner would be well advised to confine his activities to this sphere until he has gained some skill and confidence, because it is in many ways easier and less dangerous for him than faceplate jobs.

In spindle turning, scrapers should not be used. I state this quite categorically, for the action of a scraper between centres is completely wrong, Fig. 1. These tools pull and tear at the fibres leaving a terrible finish, and it would be better to give up altogether than form the habit of using them, or what is still worse, scraping with cutting tools. I say worse, because although scrapers have their uses in faceplate work, there is never any excuse for scraping with a cutting tool. As I have said, no skill is called for in the use of a scraper, and it is far more rewarding to do things properly, even if at first it is more difficult.

In schools and colleges, where the responsibility of the instructor is great, it is understandable that these tools are used, but if you really want to be a craftsman, avoid them, and use them only when you must. Over the centuries the best ways of shaping wood in a lathe have been discovered, and these are the only methods worth passing on.

The first step in spindle work is to bring the wood to a rough cylinder, this being known as roughing out, and the finish left on the wood at this stage is not critical. A gouge similar to the one in Fig. 2 is used, and the principles of using it remain the same regardless of its size. One wants to get at the rough shape as quickly as possible, in order to leave plenty of time for detail work and finishing.

Once the wood has been correctly and securely mounted in the lathe, the tool rest is brought up to the job. This raises another common question — at what height should the tool rest be set? Well, purely as a guide, I would suggest about $\frac{1}{8}$in. (3·2mm.) from the work at its nearest point, and roughly about the middle of the wood. There are times, as we shall see, when the height is critical, but this is not one of them. If it does not feel too comfortable, move it up or down a little, the optimum position will to some extent be dictated by the bevel on the gouge. Keep the tool rest close

Hour glass with three spindles, and two discs turned on woodscrew chuck

Fig. 1

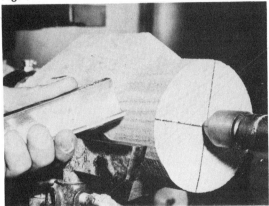

Fig. 2

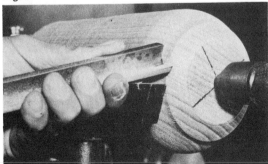

Fig. 3 (above)   Fig. 4 (below)

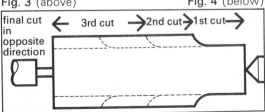

| final cut in opposite direction | ← 3rd cut | →2nd cut→ | 1st cut→ |

to the work, to give better tool control, and reduce the risk of fingers getting jammed between it and the wood. As long as it all feels comfortable, and the tool cuts nicely, the exact height does not matter too much. When the tool rest is in place, check that everything is secure, and revolve the work by hand to ensure that it will not foul the rest.

Now the lathe can be started and the roughing out begun. The gouge is held as in Fig. 3, slightly on its side, and inclined a little in the direction of the cut. Be sure that it is on the tool rest before it touches the work. The cutting is started about 2in. (50mm.) from the end of the wood, pushing the tool forward gently, and bearing in mind the fact that the bevel should form a tangent to the cutting circle. Keep the bevel in your mind the whole time you are turning, and you will have no trouble, for it is the key to the whole thing. If the handle is held too low the tool will not cut at all, if too high the action will be a scraping one and your lovely sharp edge will soon be no more. People who complain about being unable to keep an edge on the tools often fail to realise that they are using a scraping style. Run the tool along to the end, keeping your hand against the rest as a guide, and repeat the cut once or twice. Now the process can be gone through again, in stages along the job, as shown in the sketch Fig. 4. The last section will be cut in the opposite direction, so that the tool runs off the end of the wood. Starting at the end inwards is a difficult and dangerous thing for the beginner to attempt.

Fig. 1 A scraper being used on work between centres. Note the very rough finish which is nothing like as good as that produced by a gouge or chisel

Fig. 2 Working down from square to cylinder, with a roughing gouge. Note that the tool is slightly on its side, and inclined in the direction in which it is travelling

Fig. 3 Rounding over the end of a roughed out cylinder, again with the roughing gouge. Note the position in which the tool is held

Fig. 4 Stages in roughing down from a square to a cylinder. Note that cuts do not start at the ends of the wood

If the lathe is now stopped, and the work examined, it may well be found that there is a little more cutting to do before a cylinder is reached, but a few runs with the same gouge will soon put matters right. Apart from the difficulties involved in starting cuts at the ends of spindle squares, it will be appreciated that this practice could cause a long splinter of wood to be knocked off, with some danger to the turner.

Although it may not be strictly essential, try to get into the habit at all times of bringing these cylinders up as straight and true as you can, with no visible variation in diameter. It is a matter of pride, and also very good practice. If there are bumps and hollows, watch the upper edge of the work instead of the tool, and you will find things much easier. This may sound hard, but it is really no more difficult than changing gear in your car without looking at the lever.

If the gouge in use is not too large, and the intended shape is reasonably simple, it may be possible to do the entire shaping operation without changing tools, but gouges of this sort are not much use in hollows because they are ground straight across at the end. Shallow hollows are possible, but do not try deep ones, which require a spindle gouge, ground to a nose for just this purpose.

Before any attempts are made at definite projects, the basic cuts should be mastered, and practised until they come quite naturally. That may sound boring, but I do not think it will be found so. Coves, Fig. 5, are cut with a spindle gouge of suitable size in relation to the width and depth. The process is shown in the illustrations, and carried out as follows. First mark the width of the cove on wood, either with a pencil or the point of a skew chisel. If the cove is to be large, it will be started at the centre and enlarged out to the lines, but if it is a narrow one it can be started on the lines and completed in two cuts. The operation commences with the gouge completely on its side and at right angles to the tool rest, Fig. 6. It is pushed into the work and rolled over on to its back with a scooping motion, the handle being lowered at the same time, so that the cut ceases at the bottom of the hollow, Fig. 7. The process is then repeated from the opposite side to complete the cove, but until one gets used to it there is usually a little cleaning up to be done.

Fig. 5

Fig. 6

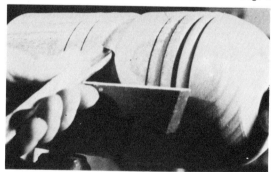

Fig. 7

Fig. 5 Cutting a cove with a small spindle gouge

Fig. 6 Commencement of cove cut. The cove has been marked, and the tool approaches the work at right angles to the tool rest, and completely on its side

Fig. 7 Position of tool at centre of cove cut. Handle has been lowered, and tool rolled on to its back

All cutting with gouges and chisels should be done downhill, or in other words from the larger diameter to the smaller, so that the tool is going with the grain. Attempts to cut uphill are likely to lead to a dig, and even if they do not the finish will be poor, as cutting against the grain always gives a rough surface. Some pupils get the idea of cove cutting right from the start, yet others find it most trying. Patience is the thing, and practice should be kept up until a number of identical coves can be cut with ease. A shape of this nature could easily be produced by pushing a scraper straight into the wood, but I suggest you try it, and compare the cut with that from a sharp gouge.

A problem which often arises with this sort of cut is that the gouge skids sideways when presented to the wood. When you are merely practising this is not too bad, but just wait until it happens right at the end of a special job, and ruins the surface! The problem can be overcome by placing the thumb on the tool rest behind the blade, and starting the cut boldly. The gouge skids simply because until it has started cutting into the wood, there is nothing for the bevel to rub on, so we are defying our golden rule. The beginner may find it helpful to make tiny grooves with the parting tool where the cuts are to start. Although small, these grooves will offer sufficient support to the bevel, and all will be well, but this will not be found necessary as proficiency is attained.

Beads are really just the opposite to coves, Fig. 8, and can be cut with various tools. There is even a tool called a beading tool which is either a wide parting tool or a narrow chisel, according to how you like to look at it. This will do the job, but then so will a small spindle gouge, and in fact the point or the heel of a sharp skew gives the best results. Small beads, like small coves, can be made in two cuts, but the larger ones are begun near the limit marks and enlarged until the described shape is arrived at, Figs. 9 and 10. The illustrations should clarify the cutting procedure, which sounds more complicated than it really is.

First we mark the size and position of the bead, as for a cove, with pencil or the point of a skew chisel. For cutting the bead you can use the heel of the skew if you like, but I find it better to use the point, because it is easier to see what is going on. When using a skew in this manner, remember that it is

Fig. 8

Fig. 9 (above)   Fig. 10 (below)

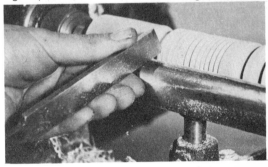

Fig. 8 Small beads being cut with a parting tool

Fig. 9 Forming a bead with the long corner of a skew chisel. It will clearly be seen that the sectional shape of the tool rest in use here is anything but suitable

Fig. 10 Finishing a bead cut. Note that the chisel finishes the cut completely on its side

the point which starts the cut, and the point alone does the cutting throughout. The process begins with the chisel at 90° to the rest, and almost, but not quite, flat on it. It will be found convenient to have the rest a little above centre for this job. The point starts the cut, and the chisel is slid along the rest and rolled over at the same time, so that its point describes an arc, finishing the cut completely on its side, point down, and still at 90° to the rest, Fig. 11. It helps if the handle is raised a little at the end of the cut. Beginners have a tendency to twist the tool too soon, so that its point does not describe a true arc, but a very rapid curve, and the result is not a bead, but a sort of inverted vee. The other half of the bead is cut in the same manner, and again plenty of practice will be needed. Softwood will do for this, or a small log or two from the woodshed. After all, why waste good timber?

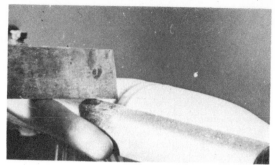

Fig. 11

The vee cut, Fig. 12, is a more simple matter. Here again the point of the skew is used, being pushed gently into the work from alternate sides, so that we start with a tiny vee and enlarge it to the desired dimensions. A word of warning here, in that the point of a chisel should never be pushed too hard into the wood. There is obviously a limit to how far it can penetrate when the cut is begun because of its shape, and any attempt to exceed this will result in the point of the tool being overheated, and the temper of the steel damaged. The skew chisel is not the easiest of tools to master, but it is certainly one of the most useful so it is worth making an effort. Keep it very sharp at all times, since this will make it much easier to handle.

Fig. 12 (above)

Fig. 13 (below)

The cut which causes more trouble than any other is the smoothing, or finishing cut, and it is a very important one. I probably get more letters on this subject than any other, so I will try to explain the technique, and just what it is that causes all the bother. The two principal points are that the bevel must rub all the time, as in any other cutting operation, and that the shaving can only come off from the part of the blade indicated, which is between the centre and the heel, or short corner. The position of the skew chisel for this cut is shown in Fig. 13, and matters will be greatly facilitated by having the tool rest high up, almost level with the top of the work.

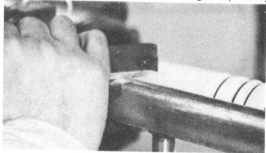

Fig. 11 Completion of a bead cut, the tool is dead square to the tool rest, and completely on its side. The handle is raised slightly at the end of the cut

Fig. 12 Skew chisel in use for vee cutting. The cut is enlarged by alternate cuts from either side, until the desired shape is reached

Fig. 13 The correct positions of chisel and tool rest for the skew smoothing cut

Here I will give you another golden rule, which is that in all skew cuts, and particularly this one, only that part of the blade which is receiving direct support from the tool rest can be used. If this is fully understood, little trouble will be experienced with the tool. You will note that, in the position shown, the tool cannot be perfectly flat on the rest, only the heel side of the blade is supported, so if the cut is taken anywhere between the centre and the long corner, there will be trouble. The idea is to get a shaving to come away, not dust, and this must be from the area of the edge indicated. If you allow the cut to get too near the centre, you are playing with fire, and conversely if the cut is right at the short corner, the tool will be pushing a lot of rubbish along in front of it, and it will be hard to see what you are doing. If the tool twists over too far, so that contact with the wood is beyond the centre point, it will be snapped down on to the rest, and the long corner will dig in.

This is so important in principle that I suggest you try it out with the lathe switched off, and a friend turning it over for you slowly by hand. Have the skew positioned so that a shaving is coming away in the right place, then gradually allow the tool to twist so that the cut goes beyond the halfway point. You will see at once what happens, far better than I, or anyone else, can tell you, and no doubt you will be able to imagine what this is like at about a thousand revolutions a minute!

Remember that in this cut, as in all chisel and gouge cuts, there must be shavings, not dust. If there is dust, then there is a wrong tool position, a blunt edge, or both, and there will be an inferior finish on the job. The cut must be a paring one, as with a knife, and if this smoothing cut is practised on scrap material until it can be done expertly, it will save the turner endless time over the years. The accepted way for a beginner to position the chisel to start this sort of cut is to place it on the work so that the edge is too far forward to cut, then draw it slowly back, raising the handle at the same time, until the cut begins. The tool can now be traversed across the wood, and after some practice, it will be found quite easy.

I often notice that pupils tend to hold the tools wrongly, perhaps through a fear of having the hands too near the work. The illustrations show that I use basically two hand positions, one over-hand, and one with the hand underneath, Figs. 14 and 15. This is not a critical matter, and the

Fig. 14 Tool held with overhand grip

Fig. 15 Tool held with hand underneath

student can please himself. What is important is that a part of the hand should ride along the tool rest to guide the cut. If the tool is held too far back, with the hands clear of the rest, there is far less control, and every chance of a dig-in.

You may sometimes wish to use this smoothing cut with the skew in a hollow, Fig. 16, and the corner of the bevel at the back may rub and mark the work. The answer is to flatten out this point on the grindstone, so that it is quite smooth, as shown in the sketch, Fig. 17.

Another rather awkward technique, until you get used to it, is the rounding over of the ends of cylinders with the skew, Fig. 18. This is worth perfecting, since it is a cut which occurs frequently in various forms, and when properly executed it can leave a finish like marble on the wood. It is per-

Fig. 16 Use of skew chisel to perform smoothing cut in shallow hollow

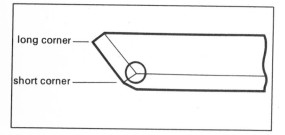

Fig. 17 Skew chisel. The area circled is flattened on the grindstone to avoid marking work when using skew in hollows

long corner

short corner

Fig. 18 Rounding over the end of a cylinder with the skew. The bevel must rub all the time, and the handle must therefore be swung as the cut proceeds

haps more awkward than the straight smoothing cut, in that the handle must be swung as the tool moves, in order to keep the bevel rubbing correctly. The principle is in other respects the same, but unless the handle is swung to keep the bevel rubbing, the tool will dig or kick, and quickly too! This is the same principle as in rolling a skew round a sphere, and if you can do that properly you have little more to learn regarding this tool.

The skew chisel excels when it comes to trimming off the ends of work, Fig. 19, because of the immaculate surface it leaves on the wood. This trimming can be done with a parting tool, but the wood will be torn about in the process, and final trimming with the skew will still be necessary, Fig. 20. In this operation only the actual point of the tool cuts, and it is vital that the rest of the blade be slightly inclined away from the wood, or there will be a nasty dig. Only light cuts can be taken, a heavy one will cause the point to overheat.

The parting tool is used a good deal in spindle work, and has its uses in faceplate work as well, but because it is easy to use, and has no bad characteristics, it is often used by beginners where other tools should properly be employed. Anyone wishing to learn the craft correctly should resist this temptation. One of its principal uses is shown in Fig. 21, in the setting out of diameters along a piece of spindle turning. Here the relevant points are marked on the wood with the aid of a pencil, and calipers are set for each diameter, from a pattern or drawing, allowing $\frac{1}{16}$in. (1·6mm.) extra for final cuts and sanding. The right and wrong ways of using this tool are quite distinct. In the wrong method the tool is pushed straight into the wood, and is in fact scraping. It will quickly lose its edge, the cut will be rough, and there will be rubbish rather than shavings. The tool is in effect a very small chisel, so it must be kept sharp and used for cutting.

When using a parting tool, the tool rest should be lowered, and the tool pointed upwards quite steeply, as in the sketch Fig. 22, so that if the handle is raised as the cut proceeds, the edge will describe an arc in its forward movement, remaining in a fixed position in relation to the axis of the work. In this manner a shaving will come away, the cut will be smooth, and the edge will last far longer. This is an interesting tool in its proper functions, and

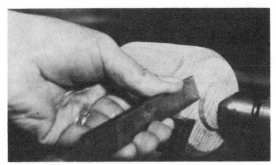

Fig. 19

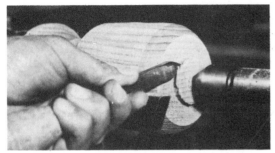

Fig. 20

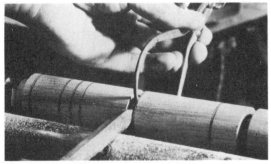

Fig. 21 (above)

Fig. 22 (below)

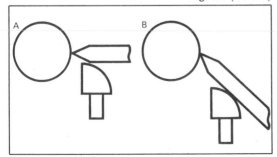

we will deal with it in more detail later, but it ought not to be used, as it often is, for bead cutting and hollowing out egg cups.

Lastly, the scraper, which as you have no doubt gathered I regard as a necessary evil. I have seen some excellent work done by scraping, and if one happens to have plenty of time, patience, sandpaper, and dust-proof lungs, it is a method which may appeal. It is not, however, good woodturning, and it takes far too long. When you must use a scraper, remember that it ought to bring off a shaving, and it will if it has been correctly sharpened. The student will be doing himself a lot of good if he restricts his use of scrapers to essential occasions, on faceplate work only.

More advanced forms of spindle work are dealt with later in the book, but I would like to touch briefly on one or two problems which are bound to arise. These are concerned with the turning of spindle work which is thin in relation to its length. One difficulty which may arise from time to time is that the work splits due to the wedge action of the driving centre. This can to some extent be overcome by the use of a four pronged centre, but the splitting may still occur, from the tailstock end, since the centre here acts as a wedge. The answer, or partial answer, is to relieve the tailstock pressure a little, but only a little, or you may create other problems, such as chatter, and of course if the work is really loose it may fly from the lathe. This splitting is really a minor matter, but there are other problems, and I doubt if any turner has ever escaped their aggravations.

Fig. 19 Trimming off across the grain on the end of turned work. The long corner of a skew is used here, only the point cuts

Fig. 20 A parting tool can be used to trim the end of the wood, but the resulting surface will be rough

Fig. 21 This photograph shows the use of a parting tool and calipers to set out diameters along a piece of copy turning

Fig. 22 Right and wrong use of parting tool. A: incorrect use—the action is a scraping one and will dull the edge. B: correct—the tool rest is lowered and the angle of the tool allows it to cut

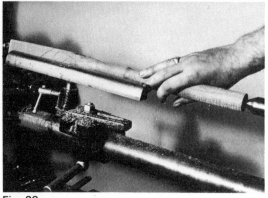

Fig. 23

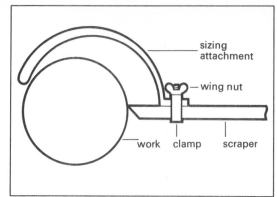

Fig. 25

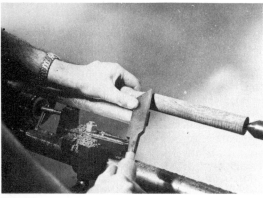

Fig. 24

Fig. 26

Fig. 23 Work which has narrow diameters is likely to whip. This can be dealt with by supporting the work by hand, or using a steady

Fig. 24 Steady the work with the left hand while using the tool with the right

Fig. 25 Work is scraped until sizing attachment drops over it. Position of attachment on the scraper blade can be adjusted as desired

Fig. 26 Correct method of using abrasive paper on turned work. Note that the paper is applied under the work, one hand being used to steady the other, and the abrasive material kept moving from side to side to avoid the formation of rings

One of these is known as whipping, and occurs on work such as is shown in Fig. 23, where a spindle turning is down to fairly narrow diameters in relation to its length. The work becomes progressively more difficult as the diameters decrease, because if allowed to do so the wood will behave very much like a skipping rope. There are two possible answers to this, one of which is to steady the work with one hand round it, whilst turning with the other, as I invariably do, Fig. 24, and the other is to use a steady. Various manufacturers supply metal ones, which are a help, but tend to mark the wood, or you can make your own, as the old turners did. None of these things is completely reliable, and where possible it is better to make up long work in sections, joining them after the turning by means of pins and sockets.

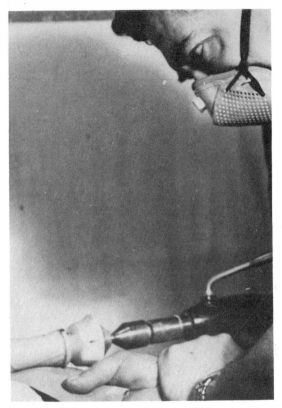

An even worse problem, as far as finding a solution goes, is that of ribbing, which is a rough spiral marking appearing round the work. It seems to have a number of causes, such as work being loose in the lathe, loose headstock bearings, work trying to climb up on to the edge of the tool, and there may be others. There are times when it cannot be overcome, and one must try to sand it out afterwards, but it is usually alleviated by supporting the work with one hand, or using a steady. Turners in the old days sometimes used leather pads, known as cotts, which they tied in place on the palm of their hands, but such things are not necessary. The skew seems to produce ribbing more quickly than any other tool, so changing to a sharp gouge may help, since the cutting action is different.

For your finishing work you will be using abrasive paper, though not too much, I hope, but please remove tool rests and holders first, for safety. The paper should be held underneath the work, Fig. 26, using one hand to steady the other. In this way the dust and rubbish goes away from you, and the paper too if it is snatched from your hand. You will also note that the fingers cannot be bent back if the work is sanded in this way. A mask, Fig. 27, should always be worn when sanding, to protect the lungs, and the paper kept moving rapidly from side to side to avoid the rings which will otherwise be scratched round the work.

Fig. 27 The use of a good mask when sanding is strongly recommended

Chapter five

The manufacture of furniture legs, which was once one of the main jobs of the woodturner, is no longer an economical proposition in view of the cheapness of mass produced items. The majority of these are made in beech, which is satisfactory for most purposes, but the turner is likely to be asked to make replacements for legs which have been damaged on antiques, and so he must know how to set about it, for these will have to be made in specified timbers. If the work is undertaken for a dealer, he will normally supply a pattern, and a piece of suitable wood, staining and finishing the article himself. The legs described here are interesting, but they take a lot of time, and some careful measuring will be needed if a good matching set is to be made. Up to this point we have had to take care to see that the work was mounted centrally in the lathe, so putting it off centre deliberately will make a change.

By means of the off-centre turning methods described in this chapter, we can make cabriole legs, club foot legs, tiny feet for jewel or trinket boxes, and oval items such as hammer handles, table lamps, or candlesticks. The processes are not difficult to follow, but they must be taken slowly, and with care, if good work is to result. The cabriole leg is not really made by turning although the foot can be turned, but a lot of hand tool work is necessary, and the wood can be held in the lathe while this is done. A good bandsaw is a blessing in this work, but if you do not possess one, a coping saw will do.

The shape of the leg is marked out on two adjacent sides of the square stock, Fig. 1, with the aid of a hardboard pattern, or by sticking on paper templates. Cutting is done carefully to the lines on one side, and the waste is put back and held in place with adhesive tape or small nails. This provides support for the blank while cutting is done to the lines on the remaining marked side, and the work is ready to go into the lathe. If required, a little extra wood can be left at the knee for carving a design. Such turning as there is in the making of these legs is done on two centres, which are marked on the blank prior to cutting out, Fig. 2. With all work of this nature particular attention must be paid to the position of the tool rest, so that it does not foul the wood. Mounting the work on centres A we shape the foot with a ½in. (12·7mm.) gouge. Mounting on centres B

Cabriole leg blank after completion of bandsaw work

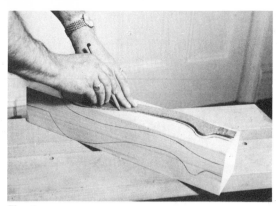

Fig. 1

Fig. 2 (above)

Fig. 3 (below)

will now permit final cuts to run the foot into the leg, and from this point on, hand tools and abrasives will provide the best means of shaping the leg and blending it into the foot, with the lathe stationary. In this sort of work the lathe should be run slowly, or there will be too much vibration.

Club foot legs are really a simple proposition, although they do not have the same appeal. They can be turned along their full length, or a square section can be left at the top for mortises, and the marking out will vary accordingly. True centres are marked at each end, and one off centre mark is made at the foot end, Fig. 3. If a square has been left at the top, the foot can be made to line up with this, or with a corner, depending on the use to which the leg is to be put. The timber used is square in section, and of a length to suit the job. If part of the leg is to be left unturned, this should be marked out clearly on the wood, but if it is to be turned along its entire length, a pin can be turned at the top to fit a hole in the table.

The first move is to put the work into the lathe between true centres, and bring it to a cylinder. The actual base of the foot is now shaped with a sharp gouge, Fig. 4, and the work is repositioned on its off centre at the tailstock end for the turning of the leg. If you are making a number of legs all alike, the height of the foot should be marked on the work before the leg turning is done. Once one becomes accustomed to the bumpy sensation caused by the wood running off centre, the turning itself is simple, taking light cuts. The foot is smoothed into the line of the leg by hand, with files and abrasives.

Small club feet can be turned up quite quickly, using a woodscrew chuck. The wood is marked at

Fig. 1 Marking out a cabriole leg blank with the aid of a pattern

Fig. 2 Centres are marked on the blank prior to cutting out

Fig. 3 How a club foot blank is prepared. Two centres are marked, one at each end, and one off centre mark at the foot

one end with its true centre, and one off centre point, Fig. 5. It is then brought to a cylinder on its true centre, and placed on the off centre for the turning of the foot. Usually there will be a pin turned on items of this nature, so that they can be accurately fitted. Fig. 6.

The turning of ovals for items such as tool handles, can be done by one of two methods, both quite simple and effective. The stock is square for the first one, and rectangular for the second. A square of beech can be used for the first exercise, with its ends trimmed dead square. The diagonals are drawn in as usual, to locate the true centres, and at each end two off-centre marks are made, one each side of the true centre mark, and about $\frac{1}{8}$in. (3·2mm.) from it, Fig. 7. These must lie on corresponding diagonals at each end, so that they are axially opposed. Mount the wood on its true centres, and bring it to a cylinder with the roughing gouge. When this has been done, it can be moved to the first pair of off-centres, and the oval turning begun. The lathe is stopped from time to time to inspect progress, and when sufficient cutting has been done, the job is moved to the other pair of off-centres and the turning completed. If the work is now returned to its true centres it can be sanded with a strip of abrasive material, with the lathe running slowly.

In the second method the marking out is different, since we are not using the diagonals, the marking takes the form of a cross, with the ends of the lines bisecting the sides of the wood, Fig. 8. Heavy black lines are drawn down the centres of the narrow sides, to be used as guides during the turning. Placing the wood in the lathe on one of the pairs of off-centre marks we turn up to the guide line, then reposition the wood on the other

Fig. 4

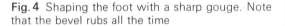

Fig. 5 (above)　　　　　　　　　Fig. 6 (below)

Fig. 4 Shaping the foot with a sharp gouge. Note that the bevel rubs all the time

Fig. 5 Small block of wood marked in preparation for turning into a club foot. Note one off centre is used

Fig. 6 Using a parting tool to turn a pin on the end of a leg

pair of off-centres and repeat the process. The true centres are now used to trim up the work with a sharp gouge, and a little sand papering will finish it off.

The items so far dealt with could come under the heading of copy turning, but this covers a wide variety of things which have to be made in pairs or sets, and of course, the replacement of a piece of furniture, or part of it. This latter can be a remunerative occupation, since it is becoming increasingly hard to find anyone who wants to take this sort of thing on, or indeed is capable of doing so. A small fireside stool is shown in Fig. 9, and the replacement of a leg for this would be a good example of the sort of thing I am talking about.

Before embarking on this, however, some thought must be given to the square parts, or pummels, which are left to carry the mortises. The mortises themselves can be cut before or after the turning, which is a matter of preference, but the cutting in where the turned part meets the square is most important. If you study legs of this sort in furniture, you will notice that the cutting in can be done in one of two ways, to give a square end to the pummels, or to make a curve, Fig. 10. Some turners use a small spindle gouge for this job, and there is nothing against it, but I prefer a skew chisel because it is more efficient, and leaves a better surface on the wood.

It is important in cutting these pummels to leave the square part intact, for it is easy to make a careless move and knock a chip off, spoiling the job. The work must be correctly marked out, and the matter of getting the wood central in the lathe is important, for if there should be any error it will show up clearly in the finished work. This very

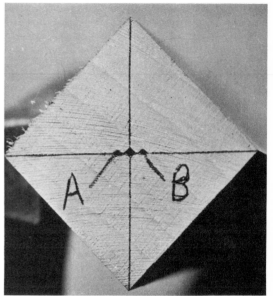

Fig. 7

Fig. 8

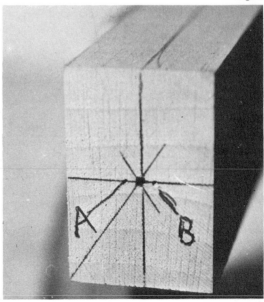

Fig 7 Marking out squares for oval turning. True centre is marked at each end, together with a pair of off centres, A and B

Fig. 8 Marking out of rectangular stock for turning into oval section. Note that lines are drawn down the centres of the narrow sides

critical centring occurs in some other operations, as we shall see, and I suggest that the old established method of knocking the wood true be employed.

Mark out the ends, and put the job between centres with light pressure. The tool rest is now positioned close to the wood at one end, and the work revolved by hand, holding a pencil, or the point of a chisel on the rest, as in Fig. 11. You can see at once whether the job is true, and if not it can be tapped in the required direction until it is. The tailstock is now tightened up, and the check repeated, just to be sure. The work will have been marked out as in Fig. 12, the parts which are to be left intact being clearly indicated, because it is quite easy to cut in the wrong place and spoil the work. Heavy black lines are marked round the wood at the points where the squares are to be cut down, and in fact if these marks are made on one face only they will still be visible when the work is revolving.

If a cut is to be made in at 90° to the rest, or in other words if a square end is wanted, the long point of the chisel is placed downwards on the rest, and the tool applied so that the bevel nearest the pummel is dead square to the job. This is an important point. Remember that it is the bevel which must be square to the work, not the blade itself. You can see this in the illustrations Fig. 13 and sketches Fig. 10. The cutting begins by raising the handle of the tool, not by pushing it at the

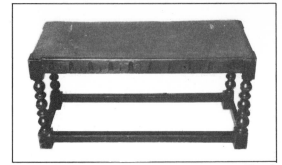

Fig. 9

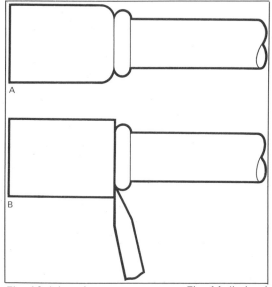

A

B

Fig. 10 (above)   Fig. 11 (below)

Fig. 9 A small fireside stool, having pummels left at top and bottom of the legs to carry mortises. This is a good example of the sort of item of furniture which the turner may expect to be called upon to repair from time to time

Fig. 10 Cutting pummels. A: curved cut. B: square cut—note the angle of chisel approach, the bevel face is square to the work

Fig. 11 Centring a square of wood in the lathe. Any inaccuracy can readily be detected, and the wood moved as required, before being finally tightened up

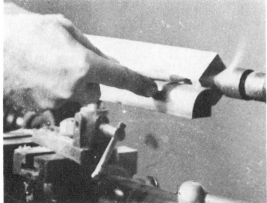

wood, and only light cuts can be made at first, or the tool will get hot. When the first cut has been made, a second is run in to meet it, Fig. 14, taking out small chips, and the process is repeated from either side alternately until the cut is continuous round the wood and the diameter is as required. Watch that the point only is used, the rest of the blade leaning a little away from the work, or there will be trouble. Plenty of practice on squares of softwood is the thing, hardwood is expensive.

If you want a rounded end to the pummels, Fig. 15 the operation is similar, the chisel being rolled in from alternate sides with the cuts finishing on the mark. Many beginners are reluctant to tackle work of this sort, feeling that the whirling corners of the wood may cause trouble, but in fact it is an easy technique to master, and a vital part of the craft. Try it with a gouge and see how you get on, but I definitely prefer the skew.

After the pummels have been cut in, the parts which are to be turned are run down to cylindrical form with a roughing gouge, and we come to the setting out of the pattern, which must obviously be done with care. A setting-out board as shown in the sketch Fig. 16 is useful, and you may like to prepare a half pattern in hardboard or plywood, so that the progress and accuracy of the job can be checked. There are proprietary template formers on the market, which are quite good, Fig. 17. These have a number of steel needles passing through a

Fig. 12

Fig. 13

Fig. 14 (above)   Fig. 15 (below)

Fig. 12 When turning furniture legs, the pummels are marked clearly with a cross, as shown, so that no mistakes are made

Fig. 13 Where the end of a pummel is required to be left square, the chisel must be held as shown here, so that it is the bevel which is square to the work, not the chisel itself

Fig. 14 Taking a second cut from the opposite side. This will result in small chips of wood being removed

Fig. 15 Showing a turned stool leg with a small pummel at the foot end which has been cut to a curve

49

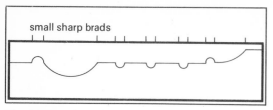

small sharp brads

Fig. 16 Board used for marking repetition work

Fig. 17 A template former, which is readily available on the market

central holder, in such a manner that they will slide independently under pressure. When the former is pressed against the master pattern both the male and female outlines are reproduced. This will certainly tell you whether you are right, but it will not really make the job much easier. Another idea which is very old, is to have a half pattern of the job attached to a board which is hinged to the bench behind the lathe, so that it can be swung up now and again for comparison.

By this time it will no doubt be clear that there is no easy way to copy shapes on a normal lathe, the answer is skill, which will come from practice, and still more practice. The marking out of the pattern can be done while the work is revolving, using a pencil or the point of a skew, but it must be done carefully. I use dividers to transfer the measurements from the pattern to the work pressing the point in lightly to make a mark. The point must trail, and not point up at the wood, or an accident is probable. Once these marks have been made, you can cut in with the parting tool, using one hand, and having a pair of calipers in the other. It may look difficult, but it is not, and you will soon be used to it.

Now the shaping can begin, using gouges of appropriate sizes, the motto being *festina lente* — or hasten slowly! Any attempt to hurry will be fatal, one needs to concentrate, and I find it hard to make a good job of copy work unless I am alone in the workshop.

Chapter six

Many furniture legs are fitted by means of a pin turned at the top, which goes into a hole. This calls for care if the article is to have strength, for it is easy to cut off that little bit too much, and spoil the job. If the leg is round, the matter is simple, but if it is square, we use the method described for cutting in on square pummels, removing the waste by means of a chisel held flat on the rest, the edge of the blade being parallel to the work, and the cut itself like that of the parting tool. The exact size of the pin is obviously critical, and a hardboard or plywood template will help a lot. I use a woodworker's vernier caliper, Fig. 1, because if this is opened so that its jaws fit the hole, the other side can be used to measure the pin, Fig. 2.

Where it is necessary to make a set of tapered legs, the blanks can be tapered in the square before turning, on the small planer, or a sawbench. It is then a relatively easy matter to turn the blank to a cylinder, maintaining the taper, and finish off with a sharp skew chisel. The experienced turner is not likely to resort to this, since it is for him a simple matter to turn the square stock to a cylinder at the maximum diameter needed, and run a parting tool in at the end, using calipers to get the diameter there. Once this has been done, he has all the guide he needs to taper the stock. Complicated jigs can be made, and they will produce tapers by scraping, but they have no appeal for the man who wants to be a woodturner. Good straight tapering will come easily with sufficient practice.

The most difficult operation on a lathe, in my own opinion anyway, is the freehand turning of a sphere or ball, but this is knack as much as anything, and can be mastered if one perseveres. The easiest approach is to make a blank as shown in Fig. 3, with the centres accurately marked on the ends and cut this out on the bandsaw before beginning the turning, Fig. 4. Heavy ridge lines are marked, and these are a great help, since they can be seen as the work is going round, Fig. 5. The ball is rough turned with a sharp spindle gouge, and two courses of action are open for the finishing. The sketches Fig. 6 will clarify this, but the first is to cut away the waste at each end, and mount the ball between two wooden cup chucks. The finishing can then be done with a sharp gouge, and with sandpaper used in a hardboard template, moving the ball around in the chucks from time to time so that all the surface is dealt with. The other way is to

A really accurate thicknesser will be invaluable when post blocking

Fig. 1

Fig. 4

Fig. 5

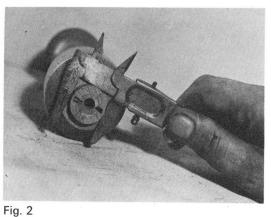

Fig. 2

Fig. 3

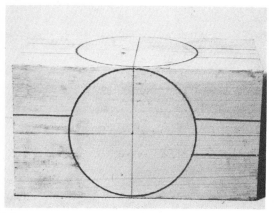

Fig. 1 Woodworker's vernier caliper being used to measure the internal diameter of the hole in the base of a table lamp

Fig. 2 The use of the vernier caliper is clear, since once the hole has been measured with the small pins, the gap between the large jaws will be exactly the same. Here the pin on the end of the lamp stem is being measured

Fig. 3 Blank marked out in readiness for bandsawing before turning a sphere

Fig. 4 Here one end of the blank has been cut on the bandsaw

Fig. 5 Blank completed and central ridge lines marked in

cut off one waste piece only, and mount the job in the lathe by driving the other one into a hollow wooden chuck. Turning is continued until you are satisfied, then the waste can be parted off, and the ball finished by hand with sandpaper, or mounted between cup chucks for sanding.

This is the method for balls of two inches and upwards, but you may wish to make a number of small ones, perhaps for a necklace, or a game of some kind. These are best turned up in short sticks,

Fig. 7, subsequently being parted off on the bandsaw and finished by hand. A piece of metal tubing of required diameter can be pushed into the revolving wood, and this is an effective way of making small spheres.

If you are making wooden beads for necklaces, which is a tiresome job, these can be sanded by placing them in a tin or drum of some kind, which is attached to the faceplate, and lined with sandpaper, or has abrasive grains loose in it, so that the

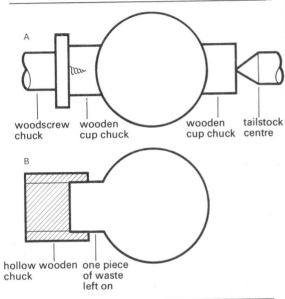

Fig. 6
Fig. 7

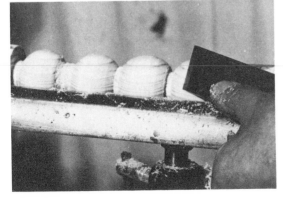

Fig. 8

Fig. 6 Methods of turning spheres from prepared blanks

Fig. 7 Small spheres or beads being turned up in short sticks

Fig. 8 Simple jig with internal taper turned up on woodscrew chuck, being used for radial drilling of sphere

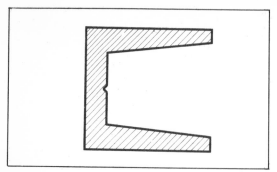

Fig. 9 Sectional view of turned jig to hold balls while they are drilled. Taper holds them firm, drill must be centred to jig

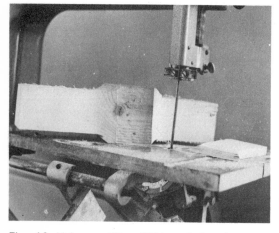

Fig. 10 Using a 15in. [381mm.] bandsaw to prepare a blank for turning a leg which has a maximum turned diameter larger than the pummels

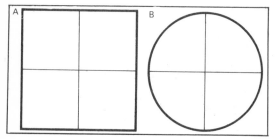

beads sand themselves while the lathe is running. Too much speed may develop sufficient centrifugal force to hold the beads still against the sides of the drum, thus defeating the whole object. The method is similar to that by which the lapidary polishes his stones.

It is sometimes necessary to drill spherical objects which are to be used as beads, feet for table lamps, and what have you, and unless the drilling is radial, the results can look bad. The best way to do this is to make a wooden jig to hold the sphere, Figs. 8 and 9, a simple enough job on the wood-screw chuck, with a taper inside it. The taper will hold the balls, and if the drill is first accurately centred to the jig, the holes will be radial. A pillar drill can be used, or a drill in the headstock and a support table on the lathe, feeding the work to the drill by hand. I made a large number of spherical candlesticks and table lamps like this once, drilling the hole for the candle or flex as described, and mounting the ball in a saucer-shaped base. If you wish to perfect your technique with the skew chisel, you will never have a better opportunity than in the turning of spheres. Once you can roll a skew round these correctly, you will not only have a first class finish, but you will have acquired a great deal of skill.

Now we come to something which will turn up again when we come to decorative turnery, this being the principle of post blocking. You may have noticed that in some table legs, the part left to carry the mortises is in fact smaller than the turned section in its main diameter. This is puzzling at first sight, but it can be arrived at in two ways. The first of these, Fig. 10, involves the bandsaw, and a considerable waste of timber, for which reason it is not likely to find many followers today. A very good bandsaw will be needed to do the cutting accurately on work of this size, anyway.

The more usual method is to post block the job, which means glueing wood round the job at the points where it is needed, and then turning. With

Fig. 11 Split turning method for table legs. A: four square pieces glued up with paper between. B: Turn as above, tapering the blank as required, and split apart

careful attention to grain the joints will be hardly noticeable, or you can make a feature of it by using wood of a contrasting colour. It sounds very simple, and so it is up to a point, but there are one or two things to watch. In order to get a really good joint, two pieces of wood are glued on to opposite sides of the core first, these being a little wider than the core itself. When the assembly is dry the pieces are trimmed back flush with a plane, or on a saw-bench as shown in the sketch Fig. 9, page 79. The resulting surface must be dead flat and true, or the joint will be no good. The second pair of blocks is glued and clamped in place and allowed to dry. The essential thing about work of this sort is that it must be centred exactly in the lathe, and the best way is to centre the core itself, before doing the building up process. This will mean taking the wood out of the lathe and putting it back, so it is a good idea to mark one fang of the driving centre with a file, and make a corresponding mark on the wood, so that the work goes back as it came out.

Another useful technique, which can be used in the making of parts for wall lamp brackets, furniture legs, parts for toys and so on, is split turning. This means, as its name implies, that the wood is in two or more pieces, held together during the turning, and split apart afterwards. There are a number of reasons for resorting to this method, among which is the provision of stock for the turning of table and standard lamps, with a hole running through it, so that little or no drilling needs to be done. If two pieces of wood are prepared with $\frac{1}{8}$in. by $\frac{1}{4}$in. (3·2mm. by 6·4mm.) groove running centrally in one side of each, they can be glued together to form a square, and turned with no trouble. To facilitate mounting the blank in the lathe, the holes at the ends may be temporarily plugged, or the grooves stopped an inch or so from the ends, and the wood drilled through afterwards. A certain kind of furniture leg can be made by this method too, four being made at once, from a blank which is glued up four square with paper between the glue joints to assist in splitting the job apart afterwards, Fig. 11. Legs made like this are, quite obviously, identical. Stock for this

must be dead square, and is best prepared over length, to allow for some screws in the waste parts for added security.

Split turning can be very useful for the making of items for the novelty trade, such as the little wall thermometer in Fig. 12, and in the construction of wall light fittings. The thermometer was made by turning in the round, splitting apart, and using a bandsaw to cut a flat surface for the dial to be stuck to.

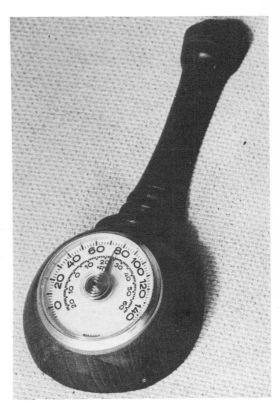

Fig.12 A small item for the novelty trade which can be made quite easily by split turning methods. A brass hook or eye is screwed into the top to finish the job

Chapter seven

One thing which causes a lot of trouble to the turner, as it does to other woodworkers, is the question of grain. It arises in getting a good surface on the work, not so much in spindle turning, but very much more with work on the faceplate. It has been said that faceplate work either cannot, or should not, be attempted with gouges, but should be scraped. This is a defeatist attitude, and no woodturner worthy of the name would agree with it.

It is not the object of this book to suggest short cuts or easy approaches, but rather to lead the student along the accepted ways. In school workshops, and even colleges, it may be best to stick to scrapers until confidence has been built up. All it is needed to know about scrapers is that they must at all times be pointed down, but the use of gouges on faceplate work calls for a fair degree of skill. There are likely to be more frustrations and disappointments here than in spindle work, but the student who tries hard enough will win in the end, and once he can do faceplate work quickly and efficiently by cutting methods, he may justly feel proud of his efforts. Shavings will pour from the tools, and he will have the great advantage of being able to get a really good finish on the work without the use of vast quantities of abrasive materials.

If trouble is experienced with the tools digging in, then just as in any other form of turning, they are either wrongly shaped, incorrectly presented to the wood, or both. The bevels must rub just as in spindle work, or trouble there will most certainly be!

Perhaps the first thing which comes to mind in connection with faceplate work is a bowl, and certainly every beginner wants to produce a well turned example. Once you can use the tools correctly on a bowl, be it large or small, you will have very little difficulty with any other form of faceplate work. The techniques of hollowing bowls, and shaping their outer surfaces, will be the same regardless of diameter, but it is as well to begin with a small one, say 6in. to 8in. (152mm. to 203mm.) in diameter, and about 2in. (50·8mm.)

The author preparing a rough disc for the turning of a bowl

deep. This can be turned on the faceplate, or on the larger of the woodscrew chucks, but which-ever method is adopted, it is vital that the mounting be completely firm, since any movement of the blank on the mounting will give rise to trouble. Any suitable sized pieces of wood can be used until proficiency is attained, and the expensive bowl turning blanks which one sees advertised should be left alone until the use of the tools becomes second nature. Firms which specialise in the construction of garden furniture often have offcuts of slab elm about 2in. (50·8mm.) thick, which is unlikely to be dry, but is excellent for practising the techniques.

Once one gets to this stage in woodturning, it becomes obvious just how useful a good bandsaw could be in the workshop. If you are serious about bowl turning, such a tool will be a wise investment, and will pay for itself in time. I said a *good* bandsaw, and this is the essence of the matter, since a poor one will be more trouble than it is worth. The thing to remember when purchasing one is that it must be able not only to accept a given thickness of wood, but to cut it with reasonable efficiency, and as far as bandsaws are concerned you will only get what you pay for. Hardwoods 3in. and 4in. (76·2mm. and 101·6mm.) thick will need to to be cut, and perhaps in quite large quantities, so you need a saw which can handle this sort of stuff well, and not be forever breaking blades. There are certain points to look for when making your choice. There should be a good machined table, which can be tilted to 45°, with guide blocks and rollers both above and below it. Power has to be adequate, and this will mean at least a half horsepower motor. The tracking mechanism must be positive in its action, or you will be forever making adjustments, and the frame of the machine should be a casting which will not flex and twist in use.

The woodturner will not be unduly worried about smoothness of cut, so it is best to use skip tooth blades, about three points to the inch. These cut rapidly, and clear their gullets better than a fine blade. I do not want to go too deeply here into the use and maintenance of bandsaws, but there is one point which crops up continually, and a few words about it may help to save the turner un-necessary bother, and so leave him more time for his turning. The thing is that a bandsaw, any bandsaw,

is only as good as the blade it is carrying at the time, and no better. The newcomer to the tool must accept that bandsaw blades are expendable, they have to be thrown away at some time or other, and it is hopeless to try to go on using one which is not fit for the job. There are so many teeth that the sharpening and setting of the blades is not worth the effort, especially in view of the fact that the biggest enemy of the bandsaw blade is metal fatigue, caused by flexing round the wheels. Even if you do sharpen and set such a blade, it is likely that it is already so fatigued as to be ready to break at any moment.

The sharpness and set of the blade are all important. Abuse of a blade can lead to the set all but

Fig. 1 A useful bandsaw for the turner's shop, with the cover removed to show wheels and blade.

Fig. 2 If the table is tilted, a bowl block can be cut as shown, saving considerable time in the outside shaping

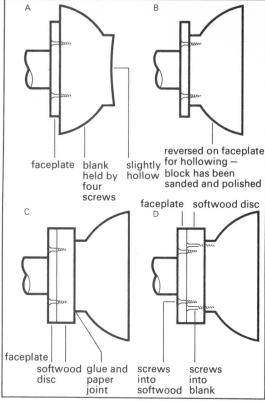

faceplate — blank held by four screws — slightly hollow — reversed on faceplate for hollowing — block has been sanded and polished

faceplate — softwood disc

faceplate — softwood disc — glue and paper joint — screws into softwood — screws into blank

Fig. 4 Various methods by which bowl blanks can be mounted and turned

Fig. 3 Marking concentric circles on the base of a bowl, in preparation for reversing it on the faceplate

disappearing, and the blade becoming overheated, and so breaking. Touching metal, whether a nail or the inside of the saw casing, often gives a condition where one side of the blade is sharper than the other. This will make the blade lead violently to right or left, and attempting to cut out a big bowl disc will be an impossible task. If the saw will not behave itself, check the settings in accordance with the manufacturer's instructions, and if this does not improve the situation, change the blade. One final thing, do not attempt to cut circles which are too small for the blade in use.

Fig. 1 shows a bandsaw with its casing removed so that the wheels can be seen. It is sometimes useful to tilt the table when cutting out bowl blanks, so that they have a sloping edge, which will save some time in the lathe for bowls of certain shapes, Fig. 2. The offcuts from these machines make excellent firewood, but it is advisable to keep them all in one place. One's wife may raid the workshop for offcuts on occasions, and it is disconcerting to find that special little block you were saving for a vase burning cheerfully in the grate!

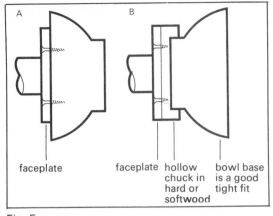

A B

faceplate

faceplate hollow bowl base
           chuck in is a good
           hard or   tight fit
           softwood

Fig. 5

Fig. 5 A: direct mounting to faceplate. The outside is turned and polished and the centre marked exactly on base B: the bowl must fit accurately into the recess

Fig. 6 Hollowing out scrap disc to take the base of the bowl

Fig. 7 $\frac{1}{4}$in. [6·4mm.], left, and $\frac{3}{8}$in. [9·5mm.], right, deep fluted long and strong gouges, used in bowl work. Note that the outside of this bowl blank has been cut with a scraper, the poor finish is obvious

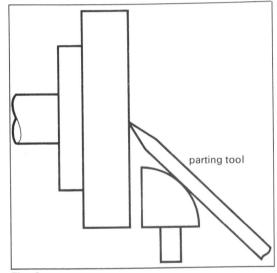

parting tool

Fig. 6

Fig. 7

The disc to be cut for a bowl should be marked out on the wood with compasses or dividers, and the centre should be indicated as clearly as possible, especially if the blank is to be kept for any length of time. Accurate centring is a big help in avoiding vibration, and there is little point in preparing a disc on the bandsaw, and then mounting it off centre. A few concentric rings on the blank can be a help when the work is mounted, as they can be seen through the holes in the faceplate, Fig. 3. As for the mounting of faceplate work in the lathe, this is almost a subject in itself, so we had better think about it at this stage.

Bowls can be turned at one mounting, without reversing them on the faceplate, and if this is intended, a disc of softwood an inch or so thick is interposed between the blank and the plate. This will effectively prevent the plate from obstructing the turning tool, which can cut into the softwood as necessary. A variation on this, which avoids having screw holes in the bottom of the bowl, is to screw the softwood disc to the faceplate, and glue the blank to it. A piece of paper can be sandwiched between to help when it has to be split apart, and a good adhesive should be used. This is a good method if you don't mind the bother of cleaning up the base afterwards. Many bowls have green baize applied to their bases anyway which hides the screw holes, and you can cut out tiny circles of rubber to stick over the screw holes. These look as though they are meant purely to protect the furniture.

A more common method in bowl work is to mount the blank on the faceplate and turn the outside. This is sanded and polished, and then the disc is reversed on the plate for hollowing. It sounds simple, but in practice it is not always easy to get the blank accurately centred when it is reversed, which results in the sides of the bowl varying in thickness.

With special bowls it is worth taking a little more trouble. By far the best way is to turn up the outside of the bowl with a direct faceplate mounting, using screws, leaving a straight-sided base about ¼in. (6·4mm.) deep. The work is now polished and removed from the machine. The next step is to take a piece of scrap hardwood, or softwood if you like, at least 1in. (25·4mm.) thick, and mount it on the faceplate, Fig. 5. A recess is now turned in this disc, which will exactly accept the base of the bowl as a drive fit. The hollowing of this is done with a parting tool, with the tool rest low, and the blade pointing up as in the sketch Fig. 6. The bowl is offered up from time to time until the base fits accurately, and the fit should be such that the bowl has to be driven in with a mallet or a block of wood. If the fit is too slack, some newspaper in the recess will help, and if you lack the courage of your own convictions you can use a little glue, but this does more for the nerves than for the job! Unless you lean too heavily on the gouge when hollowing, or have a bad dig with it, there is little chance of the work shifting.

As I mentioned earlier, speed has to be watched in bowl turning, for the peripheral speed is what we are concerned with, and on a large bowl disc this can be very high. If it is too high the turning will be extremely difficult, and the tools will become overheated. There is also the matter of vibration, which can be really alarming on a big blank if the speed is excessive. Bowls up to 8in. (203·2mm.) or so in diameter will give no trouble on a normal lathe, but for the big ones some form of speed reduction will be needed. It is possible to run the lathe too fast in any form of turning, and some beginners fail to

Fig. 8 Beginning the shaping of the outside of the bowl blank, using a ⅜in. [9·5mm.] long and strong gouge, on its side, and with the handle held low so that the bevel can rub. The shavings are typical of the tool

realise this when using drill-driven attachments powered by a single speed drill doing about 3,000 r.p.m. The speed should be fast enough to get a good finish, but slow enough to let the tools cut. If your lathe has a gearbox, as mine has, all is well, but if not you will have to use a countershaft to bring the speed down to 500—600 r.p.m. With luck, the vibration will disappear when the blank has been trued up, but such is not always the case since the wood itself may not be in perfect balance, due to the presence of heartwood and sapwood. If you are lucky enough to get a blank which has a strip of light coloured sapwood at one side, however, it can look most attractive.

If the blank has been mounted with screws, care must be taken in the hollowing, and the depth checked from time to time. If you go too deep there will be a nasty rattle as the tool strikes the screw points, which will not help the job or the tool, and is another reason for using the hollow chuck method.

Tools for bowl work, as for any other form of turning, must be kept razor sharp, or they will be overheated, and the finish will not be good. I use a ⅜in. (9·5mm.) deep long and strong gouge for most bowl work, Fig. 7, aided and abetted by a round nosed scraper, and ½in. or ¼in. (12·7mm. or

grain, thus giving the best possible finish to the wood, Fig. 9. When the desired shape has been cut, the lathe should be stopped so that the work can be examined closely. It may well be found that there is roughness in two places on the edge of the blank, where the tool has been cutting on the end grain, Fig. 10. This is one of the real problems of bowl work, but once you are master of the gouges you will be able to deal with it quite easily. Sometimes a few light cuts with a freshly sharpened scraper will help matters, but the best bet by far is to take a small but very sharp gouge, well on its side with the bevel rubbing, so that it gives a paring cut. Have the tool rest close to the

Fig. 9 A $\frac{1}{4}$in. [6·4mm.] gouge being used for final cuts on the outside of a bowl blank, to remove roughness on the end grain. The bevel must rub

Fig. 10 A good example of roughness across the grain on elm, and two very sharp gouges which will be used to remove it

6·4mm.) half round gouge ground to a nose, the latter for dealing with end grain troubles.

Now for the turning. When I buy planks for bowl discs I get the timber yard to put them through a planer, so that both faces are flat and parallel, but if this has not been done, the disc must be mounted, its face trued up with a gouge or scraper, and made very slightly hollow so that it sits well on the face-plate, and then reversed. The other face can now be trued up, and a few light cuts on the edge will give you a true disc which should be ready for turning. The photographs will help to show how the tools are used. The bevel of the bowl gouge must rub like that of any other tool, and you will note that it is ground short. If it were not, the handle would need to be held very low, which would be awkward. This tool is used on its side at all times, never on its back.

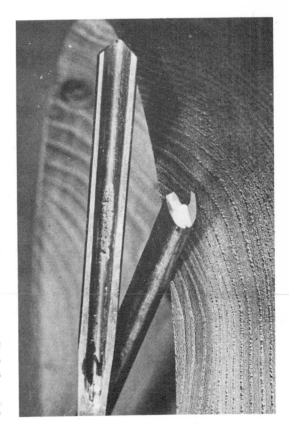

The outside of the bowl can now be shaped according to individual taste, and the base formed with the parting tool, or the corner of the gouge, which gives a cleaner cut. The shaping of the outside is done as in Fig. 8, and if you are doing it correctly, with a sharp gouge, the heaps of shavings on the floor should be very satisfying. There should be little or no dust. The cutting is done towards the headstock, so that it is with the work. The cuts should be light, and if properly executed they will usually remove the roughness. Should it persist, as it sometimes will, the lathe can be stopped, and the work sanded against the lie of the fibres.

An old and tried way of dealing with rough end grain is to fit a reversing switch to the lathe so that the work can be made to run backwards. The tool rest and holder are removed, and a few light cuts are taken with a sharp scraper, held upside down and pointing upwards, so that its edge is trailing on the work, Fig. 11. The tool rest is not used, but be careful about this reversing business, which I am not personally recommending and, in fact, never do myself. It can cause the faceplate to unwind itself from the mandrel, and it should only be done on the outside of a bowl, never inside.

When you have finally satisfied yourself that the outside is as good as you can get it, the blank can be reversed for hollowing, Fig. 13, which will not take long if done as follows.

If you hollow bowls entirely by scraping methods, you will not get very many made, in fact it could take most of the day to make one! The bowl gouge will slice out thick shavings, and have the job done in no time. You could perform the hollowing operation by starting in the middle and working your way out, or by starting at the outside and taking sweeping cuts in to the centre but both these methods have one disadvantage, which is that as the wall of the bowl becomes thinner, it has no support, so it bounces under the tool, and makes things difficult. You can turn with one hand (or can you?) and press a handful of shavings against the outside as a damper, but this is not really necessary. It is much better to begin the

Fig. 11

Fig. 12

Fig. 11 Illustrating a method which some turners like to use to get rid of roughness on the outside of bowls. As the direction of rotation has been reversed, care is needed to see that the faceplate does not unlock from the mandrel

Fig. 12 The corner of a bowl gouge being used to form the base part of a bowl. This can be done with the parting tool, but the finish will not be as clean

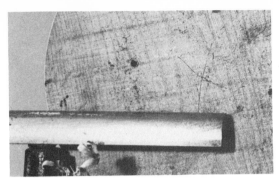

Fig. 13

Fig. 14

Fig. 15 (above)

Fig. 16 (below)

hollowing one third of the way in from the edge, cutting alternately from each side, Figs. 14 and 15, so that there is still a fair sized lump of wood left in the centre when the walls are completed, effectively damping out the vibration, Fig. 16. This central hump is removed last, with light cuts, Fig. 17 taking care to see that the gouge does not go past the centre, or it will be lifted up and flung back down on to the rest with some force, Fig. 18.

If you have difficulty in starting the hollowing because the gouge skids, you can make a little cut with the parting tool to support the bevel for the first cut. Once the hollowing is under way each cut can be started by making a small step with the corner of the gouge, Fig. 19. This will prevent skidding, and make the job simpler, though you will not find it necessary when you get used to the work. It may or may not be possible to complete the hollowing with the gouge alone, depending on the inside shape, but if the gouge cannot follow all the way round, a scraper can be used for the final cuts, as long as it is sharp, and not pushed too hard into the wood. If too much pressure is applied to it the wood will be torn, and you will have a real problem on your hands, Fig. 20.

A practice which has grown in popularity in recent years is that of turning bowls from wet elm. It has its advantages, and is quite a pleasant occupation. Moisture is flung out in some

Fig. 13 The bowl blank has been shaped on the outside, and reversed on the faceplate ready for hollowing. Note the holes left by the screws in the original mounting

Fig. 14 The hollowing of the bowl commences about one third of the way in from the edge, cuts being taken from alternative sides. The tool is on its side at all times, with the bevel rubbing the work

Fig. 15 Cutting down on the bowl wall. Keep the tool very sharp

Fig. 16 It will be seen here that a considerable lump of wood is left at the centre of the bowl, help-ing greatly to stop vibration and drumming

Fig. 17

Fig. 18

Fig. 19 (above)

Fig. 20 (below)

quantity by centrifugal force, so it is as well to stand a little to one side. Wet wood turns very much better than dry, so you will have lovely piles of shavings all over the place, which is good for the ego. There seems to be a misapprehension among beginners that there is some mystic virtue in long shavings, the reason for which eludes me. I am constantly being asked how to get them, and I usually suggest wet wood, but they are of purely academic interest to me. The whole point is that if you are getting shavings, you are doing things right—the length of them is irrelevant.

Bowls turned from wet elm—which can be as green as you like—are not turned in one operation. The method is to turn them on a large woodscrew chuck, shaping the outside and hollowing the inside so that they are left 1 in. (25·4mm.) or more thick, complete with central core so that they can later be replaced in the lathe. They are then hung up in some netting in a dry airy place, or put into the airing cupboard and left for a week or two. They will distort and shrink across the grain, but they will not normally split. When they have dried they can be replaced in the lathe and finished off, but you may have to plane the bases true before remounting them. You could try turning one or two to completion, with thin walls, and varnishing them before giving them the drying treatment, which can produce surprising results.

Fig. 17 The walls have been brought to the required thickness, and the gouge is now employed in removing the central core

Fig. 18 Here the small piece of wood left at the centre of the bowl is indicated by a screwdriver. When removing this, great care must be taken to see that the gouge does not pass the centre mark

Fig. 19 Forming a small step on the central core to support the gouge at the start of its next cut

Fig. 20 If it is found necessary to use a scraper for the final cuts inside the bowl, it must be sharp, pointed downwards, and little pressure used on it

The finishing of turned work, polishing, and the use of waxes and sealers is dealt with in Chapter 13, but do not discard blanks merely because they have knots or blemishes. These can sometimes be attractive in the finished article, but wood with loose knots, splits, or faults which could be dangerous should never be used. Sometimes, when using a gouge or scraper to hollow a bowl, it may be found hard to hold the tool steady, which is usually due to the wood being harder in one place than another. The tool should be held firmly, with the rest close up to the cutting point, and I rest my elbow on the tailstock, but I take the centre out first!

The problem of roughness across the grain is not confined to the outer surfaces of bowls, it can crop up on the inside too, and frequently does. The whole thing can be a nightmare to the student in his early days, but he may find comfort in the fact that it happens to everyone. The degree of severity varies with the timber in use, some being far worse than others. I recall that years ago, after struggling with this phenomenon for a long time, I solemnly carried a half finished bowl into the house and placed it gently on the fire. This procedure did nothing for my ability as a woodturner, but it improved my temper a great deal! There is no need for despondency however, anyone who tries hard enough will ultimately get the knack, and the sense of achievement is considerable.

Fig. 21 (above)

Fig. 22 (below)

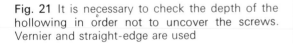

Fig. 21 It is necessary to check the depth of the hollowing in order not to uncover the screws. Vernier and straight-edge are used

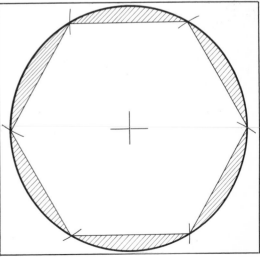

Fig. 22 Laminated bowl with hexagonal centre— the shaded parts are waste. A circle is drawn on the wood and the radius stepped out round it with compasses. The hexagon is then marked, sawn out on the bandsaw, and each face is skimmed on a planer. Contrasting strips of wood are glued and cramped on to the six faces, and when the glue is completely dry, the bowl can be turned

Chapter eight

There is one big advantage in the turning of bowls, in that they are wide in relation to their depth, and so you can see what is happening all the time. This is not the case with biscuit barrels, tobacco humidors, tea caddies, and vases. These are deep, and there is not much chance of seeing anything without stopping the lathe, and clearing out the rubbish. It is not advisable for a beginner to use gouges on such work, since he will not be able to see what the bevel is doing. The cutting edge has often to be some distance from the support of the tool rest, and control of the tool becomes difficult, to say the least. Some of the items mentioned can be made by built up or laminated methods, but this is dealt with in Chapter Nine. For the moment, let us consider the turning of a tea caddy and a small vase, both from the solid.

For the vase use a block of wood 3in. (76·2mm.) square and about 6in. (152·4mm.) long, with its ends cut off dead square. Any hardwood will do. A hole is first drilled in this to the required depth, using as large a cutter as possible, Fig. 1. If you have a 2in. or 2½in. (50·8mm. or 63·5mm.) forstner pattern, or a sawtooth bit, either will do admirably, but I do not possess such luxuries so I have used a wing bit, Fig. 2. The speed of the lathe must be kept low during the drilling, or an expensive cutter will be burned and ruined. The drilling can be done with the wood mounted on the large woodscrew chuck and the bit in the tailstock, or with the bit held in a chuck on the mandrel and the wood fed to it. In the latter case the wood is held by hand, which is quite safe, and the feed is by means of the tailstock. This allows a steady feed, and the hole will be true.

When this operation has been completed, the tool rest is positioned across the front of the work, and the neck of the vase opened out with a parting tool or sharp scraper, taking very light cuts, or the blank may be loosened on the chuck, Fig. 3. Now make a small tapered wooden plug, Fig. 4, fit this into the neck, and bring the tailstock up to give support, Fig. 5, while the outside of the vase is shaped. A ¾in. (19·1mm.) gouge, on its side with the bevel rubbing will do this little job very well, Fig. 6. Vases can be hollowed out to take various types of glass liner, but if you do not want to do

A small vase in sycamore

Fig. 1

Fig. 2

Fig. 3

this, you can waterproof the vase by pouring in molten candle wax, and pouring it out again before it sets. Be careful in melting the wax, or it may ignite. The hot wax will penetrate into the wood, and make it waterproof for quite a long time.

As an alternative to the cutters suggested above for drilling the blanks, ordinary carpenter's bits can be used, but the square part must be cut off, and the thread of the lead screw filed smooth so that it does not draw into the wood.

The tea caddy is rather a different proposition, in that it will have a fitted lid, is considerably deeper than the vase, and must have clean, straight sides internally as well as externally.

The lid can, if you like, be recessed on the outer face, to take a small ceramic tile, or other decoration. My block of wood was 4in. (101·6mm.) square and 9in. (228·6mm.) long, both lid and caddy being made from it. Some tractable timber like sycamore, lime, or beech should be used, the job is tricky enough without picking an awkward wood. Mount the blank centrally in the lathe, and run it down to a cylinder, taking your time, and making sure that it is straight and true. Nice curly shavings should be coming away now, not dust. When you are satisfied, raise the tool rest up almost level with the top of the work, and run a smoothing cut along with a sharp skew.

A check with calipers at this stage will show if the work is constant in its diameter, and if it is you can proceed. Measuring 6½in. (175·1mm.) along the work from the headstock end, scribe a mark to indicate the length of the caddy itself, then lower

---

Fig. 1 A large wing bit being used at low speed to drill a hole in a small block in preparation for vase turning. The block is held in the mortising attachment of the machine

Fig. 2 The shape of the bit used. A saw tooth pattern would do equally well

Fig. 3 The work is now mounted on a woodscrew chuck, and the tool rest positioned across the front for opening out the neck

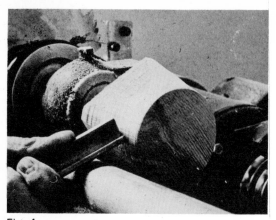

Fig. 4

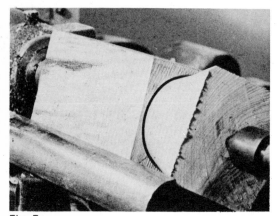

Fig. 5

Fig. 6

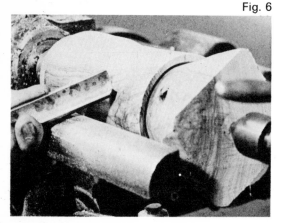

the tool rest and back the tailstock centre off just a fraction, as is always done when a parting tool cut is to be made really deep into the work, to prevent the work collapsing and jamming the tool. With the tool handle low and the edge really sharp, go in to about ¼in. (6·4mm.) from the centre, then remove the work from the lathe, and complete the parting off with a handsaw. The small piece, which will later form the lid, will not be needed for a while, until you have done most of the work on the container.

The longer part is now mounted on a large wood-screw chuck, using two extra screws in the holes provided, and making sure that the fixing is really firm. Hollowing of the type now faced is not so much difficult as tricky, and what you need most is confidence. The beginner is advised to go gently, yet be positive in what he does, for he will be working by feel most of the time. Again, as with the vase, drill a hole to the required depth, Fig. 10. If you like you can go in with a thin drill first, to help keep the bigger one straight, but I doubt if it is worth the trouble. A piece of adhesive tape round the drill will do as a depth marker, and if you find that the chuck prevents the drill from going to the full depth, the opening can be enlarged with a parting tool or scraper so that the nose of the chuck can enter. When you are happy about the hole, take the tailstock away, and remove the bit, or you may jab your arm on it.

The tool rest is now put across the front of the job and the hollowing is begun with the parting tool, Fig. 11. It is important not to disturb the work on its mounting, and you will get on better if you push the tool straight in rather than hold the handle low, taking cuts about half the width of the blade.

Fig. 4 Shaping up a small wooden plug to fit the neck, so that the tailstock can be brought up

Fig. 5 Plug fitted to blank, and tailstock brought up with revolving centre, to support the job during the shaping of the outside

Fig. 6 Roughing down the square to a cylinder, before shaping with a small spindle gouge

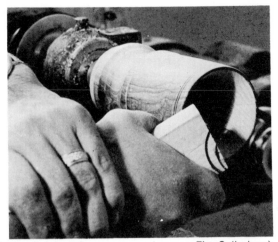

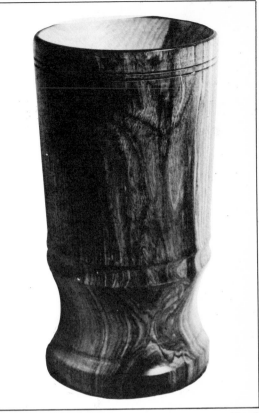

Fig. 7 (above)   Fig. 8 (below)

Fig. 7 Blackening the edge of the small vase, by means of pressure from a piece of scrap wood

Fig. 8 Burnishing the job after sanding, with a handful of shavings

Fig. 9 The finished vase. In this case polishing has been done with Carnauba wax

Fig. 9

The parting tool will get you started, but it will not do the whole job, and there is a legitimate case here for grinding up a special tool from an old file. The one I use, Fig. 12, is just right, having an edge to cut in the bottom of the hole, and one to clean the side as it goes in. It is long and strong enough for the job, even though it has to work with a lot of projection over the tool rest. The tool will become more difficult to handle as the cavity deepens, and if you can get the tool rest, or part of it, into the hole it will help.

You are unlikely to be able to see anything at all, since the shavings and general rubbish cannot get away, and it will be necessary to stop from time to time and clean them out, so that progress can be inspected. It is not wise to take the walls right down to final thickness at this stage. A freshly sharpened tool should be used for this, with very

Fig. 10

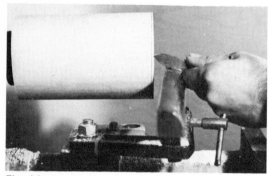

Fig. 11

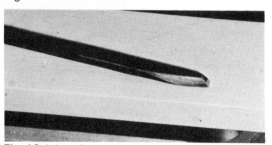

Fig. 12 (above)

Fig. 13 (below)

light cuts, and the wall thickness should be constant to the bottom of the cavity. Sand the inside carefully now, and the worst is behind you.

The piece of wood for the lid is now mounted in place of the main part, and trimmed back with the parting tool to a length of 1½in. (38·1mm.). Be careful that the screws used in the chuck are not long enough to come right through the work. If you are intending to put a tile in the top, the recess for this can be cut now. Draw round the tile to give an indication of the size for the recess, and hollow carefully with the parting tool, working out to the line, and stopping the lathe to check until you have a good fit. Sand this face carefully, and mark the centre with a bradawl, then the wood can be reversed on the chuck. It will be seen that there is a double rebate at the edge, to fit the lid to the caddy, and leave a finger grip for ease of removal. Take a couple of light cuts with a gouge across the edge of the work, in case it has gone a little off centre in reversing, and cut in as in Fig. 13 to get the fit of the lid, the rebate being ¼in. (6·4mm.) wide. Trial and error is the thing, and go gently, or too much will be taken off and the fit will be sloppy. You want a fairly tight fit at this stage, easing it with sandpaper when the job is finished.

The inside of the lid is now shaped with a sharp scraper or a small gouge, the second rebate is cut for the finger grip, then caddy and lid are fitted together, and the tailstock brought up to give support. Using a skew chisel which has just been sharpened, or a gouge if you feel cowardly, take one or two light cuts along the job, to unite lid and caddy as a perfect fit. Sandpaper now if you must, but if that skew was sharp you will hardly need to.

Fig. 10 Pre-drilling the tea caddy blank by means of a bit held in a chuck in the tailstock, this being fed to the work by means of the handwheel

Fig. 11 Opening up the hole with a parting tool

Fig. 12 Special tool ground up for deep hollowing. Note the shape, and the cutting edge across the end and along the left hand side

Fig. 13 Rebating the lid in readiness for fitting to the body

A good burnish with some soft shavings, and the job is ready for whatever finish you wish to apply, but the inside is best left bare. A spot of glue will fix the tile in place, and there you are.

The boring of holes through table and standard lamps, to take the flex, is a simple enough job if you have the right equipment. There is not much problem in the case of normal table lamps, which are fairly short, since these can be hand held and fed to a boring bit in the headstock by means of the tailstock handwheel, reversing to complete the job. Longer holes, however, call for special tools, which are available for most lathes. The outfit shown here is for a Coronet Major, and consists of a shell auger, an attachment for the tool rest holder which has a ring centre threaded into it, a spike shaped centre finder, and a counter-boring tool. These long holes can be drilled before or after the turning, but I prefer to turn and polish the lamps first. The system is straightforward, although it is hard not to make it sound complicated, and is carried out as follows. First the tailstock centre is removed, and the centre finder fitted in its place, Fig. 14. The attachment with the ring centre is now fitted to the tool rest, with the ring centre screwed right home, Fig. 15. A little adjustment will now enable the centre finder to be passed through the ring centre, Fig. 16, and into the end of the wood.

When this has been done, the wood is tightened in the lathe by the tailstock, to give the driving centre a grip, and the tool rest holder and attachment are clamped in position. The saddle is then slid along so that the ring centre touches the end of the work, and the ring centre is screwed out by means of a

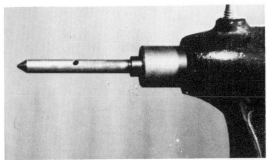

Fig. 14

Fig. 15

Fig. 16

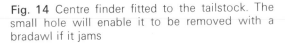

Fig. 14 Centre finder fitted to the tailstock. The small hole will enable it to be removed with a bradawl if it jams

Fig. 15 Ring centre attachment fitted to tool rest holder. The small wing nut at the top clamps the centre at any set position

Fig. 16 With all clamps slack the tailstock is slid forward so that the centre finder passes through the ring centre attachment

Fig. 17

Fig. 20

Fig. 18 (above)

Fig. 19 (below)

Fig. 17 Tailstock and lathe saddle are now slid forward so that ring centre touches work, and centre engages in hole left by revolving centre. Clamps are tightened, and ring centre screwed out to bite into wood

Fig. 18 A spot of oil on the ring centre will prevent burning

Fig. 19 The drilling can now commence by passing the auger through the ring centre attachment, tailstock and centre finder having been removed

Fig. 20 At no time should the auger be pushed into the wood more than the length of its shell. It is then withdrawn and the dust emptied

Fig. 21 This is continued until the halfway mark has been passed, when the work is reversed to complete the drilling

Fig. 22 Counterboring tool fitted to mandrel. The pin will locate the work centrally, whilst it is driven by the fangs

Fig. 23 Angle drilling for stool legs, etc. The work is fed to the cutter in headstock by sliding the saddle along the lathe bed

Fig. 21

Fig. 22 (above)

Fig. 23 (below)

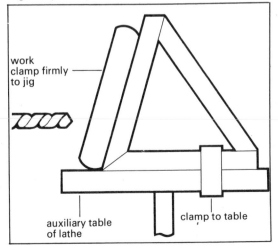

work clamp firmly to jig

auxiliary table of lathe

clamp to table

tommy bar so that it bites into the work, Fig. 17. It should now be taken back half a turn to relieve the pressure, and a drop of oil applied where it contacts the work, to prevent burning, Fig. 18. The clamp of the ring centre can now be tightened and the tailstock and centre finder withdrawn.

The lathe is now started at about 1,000 r.p.m., and the auger fed steadily into the wood through the ring centre. These augers cut well if they are sharp, but if not they will overheat. Go in to the depth of the shell, Fig. 19, but no more, then remove and empty the dust, Fig. 20. This is repeated until the halfway mark is passed, Fig. 21. The wood is now reversed to complete the job, but the driving centre is removed, and the counterboring tool fitted in its place, Fig. 22. This has a pin to fit the hole made by the auger, and so centralises the work, whilst its blade-like fangs drive the wood. The pin in this device can be removed by unscrewing an Allen screw, and the tool is then used to bore 1in. (25·4mm.) holes in lamp bases to take the pin which is turned on the stem. I never bother to do this because it seems quicker to make these holes with a parting tool while the base is being turned.

A point worth noting is that the ring centre in the attachment is the same size as an ordinary tailstock ring centre, so if you use one of these when turning the lamps, there will be no need to use the centre finder, since there will be a ready-made location for the attachment. I realise that all this sounds complicated, but the photographs will make it clear, and it is quite simple. Once you have used the tools a few times there will be nothing to it.

Sometimes it may be necessary to drill holes at set angles, as for example to fit legs to a three legged stool. A wooden jig can be made as in the sketch Fig. 23, to hold the work on either the mortising attachment of the lathe, or on an auxiliary table. This makes the job simple, but the work must be firmly clamped. If the mortiser is used its depth stop can be employed, but if you use a table, a 'G' cramp on the lathe bed will serve the same purpose.

At one time I used to make numbers of wine tables, having a turned central pillar and three small legs

Fig. 24 A simple method of using a circular saw-blade on a universal machine to divide work equally, the tool rest being used as a ruler to mark the wood

Fig. 26 Lathe saddle is slid along so that the drill passes through the jig, the resulting hole being at centre height

Fig. 25 Small jig turned up from scrap wood for radial drilling

at the base. For this it was necessary to drill radial holes for dowels in the base of the pillar, which had to be equally spaced. I did the marking out for this with a template, but if your lathe has an indexing head so much the better. An idea which has various applications with machines like the Major is to make a metal disc about 10in. (254mm.) in diameter, with a central hole the same size as the one in the saw blade, or you might get away with using plywood. The idea is to drill holes at set intervals around this so that they are equally spaced, and fit the disc in place of the sawblade, projecting through the table. If a pin is pushed through one of the holes, and brought down to rest on the table, a line can be drawn along the work, using the tool rest as a ruler. If the pin is moved to another hole, and the process repeated, it will be possible to divide the work equally. This sort of thing is useful when a turning has to be fluted.

Some users of machines of this type use a coarse toothed sawblade as a dividing head, treating the gullets as though they were holes in a disc, and putting a peg in them, Fig. 24. The drilling of holes into turned work so that they are truly radial is no problem. A small piece of wood is turned up as in Fig. 25, and fitted firmly into the tool rest holder. Now a drill of the required size is put into a Jacobs chuck on the mandrel, and the wooden jig lined

up centrally with it, Fig. 26. If the tool rest holder is slid along so that the revolving drill passes through it, it is obvious that the hole in the wooden pin is at centre height, Fig. 27. Now move the saddle out of the way, and mount the work between centres. If the jig is lined up with the point at which the hole is to be drilled, an electric drill can be used, and the hole will be quite accurate, Fig. 27.

Fig. 27 With the tool rest holder swung round to the outside of the work, an electric drill is used to drill through the hole in the jig, so that the holes in the work are radial

Chapter nine

I should perhaps make it clear before embarking on this chapter that the subject of decorative turnery is material enough for a book on its own, so I can hardly do justice to it here. On the other hand, I may be able to arouse the interest of the student in this branch of the craft, and once he has started, he will invent his own variations. I have concentrated on the basics of laminated, post blocked, and segmental assemblies, some of which can be extended and combined to make very intricate patterns. In all work of this nature the joints must be perfect, the wood properly seasoned, and only the best adhesives used. If this is adhered to there is no need for built-up assemblies to disintegrate during the turning, since the glues which are available today are immensely strong. Every built-up blank must, however, be given a thorough examination prior to mounting in the lathe, and if there is room for doubt it should be discarded. Proper cramping is essential and for the sake of safety all build-ups should be given at least two days at room temperature to allow the adhesive to cure. Mahogany with lime or sycamore will give a good colour contrast, and in fact a lot of my work is done with mahogany and ordinary deal. It is said that the woods must be of equal hardness, and perhaps this is advisable for the beginner, but do not be afraid to experiment.

One of the easiest forms of decorative turnery is the straightforward laminated blank, in which strips of wood of contrasting colours are glued together to make striped boards, which can be cut on the bandsaw to give bowl or lamp base discs, Fig. 1. Rings of wood of alternate colours can be cut with a jigsaw, and glued up in a pile to make blanks for biscuit barrels, string boxes, and so on. The grain in each layer of this sort of construction should be arranged to alternate, to give stability to the finished job, and with the strip method it helps if the heart sides alternate, Fig. 2.

Another very common form of decorative work, which has many variations, is the construction of discs from wedge shaped pieces of alternate light and dark wood, Fig. 3. If you wish you can use

Fig. 1 Small bowls made by laminating strips of wood side by side with the colours alternating, then cutting to discs on a bandsaw and turning in the normal manner

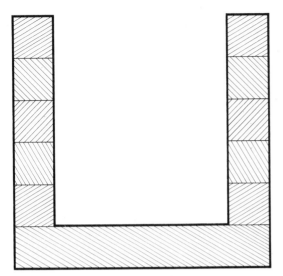

Fig. 2 Sectional view of built-up blank made from rings

Fig. 3 A lamp base being made from a laminated blank, with alternate coloured woods

wedges which are all the same colour, inserting thin spacers of a lighter or darker colour between them, Fig.4. The cutting angle of the wedges will not be affected by this, but the diameter of the disc will be increased, and there will be a hole in the centre which can either be plugged, or ignored if it will not be visible in the finished job. A good example of this would be a lamp base, where the hole would in fact be useful in getting the flex through. The angle required in the outer corners of these wedges can be arrived at simply by dividing the number of segments into 180. The mitre setting for the sawbench can be obtained by deducting this figure from 90, so a ten-sided assembly would need a mitre setting of 18°, or a sawtable tilt of 72°. A hollow ground or novelty blade is used to cut the pieces, and it is better by far to avoid sanding the edges if you can. The cramping, which is important, is often done by putting wire round the work and twisting this tight with a piece of wood— the old Spanish windlass in fact. This works, but I prefer to use large screw type clips, which I undo and join together to get the size I want.

Any good quality wood glue can be used, but some set very hard, so it is as well to wear goggles, or some form of eye protection.

Wedges for this sort of work are normally crosscut from strips, Fig. 5, in which case the grain will run round the blank, and there will be no trouble with end grain in the turning. An alternative is to tilt the saw table, and rip off bevelled lengths of wood from the plank, which are then cut to size. With an assembly made from these the grain will be vertical, so that there will be end grain on the faces of the blank. By using 90° triangles instead of the normal wedge shape, you can get odd effects, since these will produce a spiral look on the blank, which can be interesting when turned, Fig. 6. Alternatively, if the wedge shaped lengths of wood are crosscut on their backs at an angle, this will give a spiral effect on the side of the blank. Small blanks made up in this way are very useful for making table lighters and lamps.

A popular way of making table lamps, by which one can arrive at some intricate patterns, is post blocking, which I mentioned earlier on page 54, but extreme care must be taken both in assembly and in getting the blank central in the lathe if good results are to be achieved. Make the central core

Fig. 4

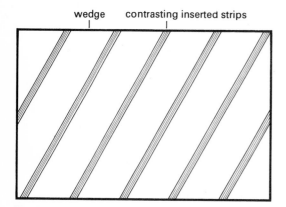

wedge   contrasting inserted strips

Fig. 5

Fig. 6

dead square throughout, and centre it exactly, checking by running a parting tool cut in at the ends, Fig. 7. Any error must be corrected now, or the rest of the work will be a waste of time. It is convenient to make up a number of these cores at a session, some light and some dark; they are always useful. As in some other jobs, there should be a mark filed on one fang of the driving centre, and a corresponding pencil mark on the core, so that this can be put back as it came out. Even the very slightest error will show in the finished job. Fix the first two laminations to opposite sides, with a slight overhang, and trim them back true when set, Figs. 8 and 9. The next two layers now go on, and the process is repeated according to the desired design, Fig. 10.

In bowl work there are various ways of providing a little decoration, two popular ones being the insertion of contrasting plugs in the periphery of the bowl, either right through the wood or partly so, and the inlaying of strips of wood round the bowl, which can be most effective. The plugging is done in a similar manner to that described for the drilling of radial holes in turned work, the bowl being suitably divided round the edge, Figs. 11 and 12, and the drilling done with the bowl mounted in the lathe, using our home-made radial drilling jig. The plugs could be dowel, but this will give end grain on the surface, which is not too good. They are best cut with a plug cutter, Fig. 13, and left a little proud of the surface. Once they have completely set, and not before, they can be trimmed flush with a sharp gouge, and the job can be polished.

Fig. 4 A blank made up for turning, using wedges of wood with spacers of an alternative colour. Note the use of rubber hose clips as clamps. Spacers increase diameter of disc, and cause hole at centre

Fig. 5 Triangular lengths of wood crosscut at an angle on their backs can be assembled as above

Fig. 6 Partially turned blank made up of right-angled triangles. The spacers are of oil tempered hardboard, and it will be noted that the triangles run to the edge of the central hole, rather than to the centre

Fig. 7

Fig. 8

Fig. 9

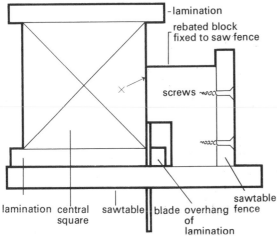

Fig. 10

Fig. 7 Method of centring central cores for post blocked work by trimming the ends with a parting tool, any error is obvious

Fig. 8 Further stages in the construction of post blocked blanks. Note that the first pairs of blocks which are glued on should be very slightly wider than the core, subsequently being trimmed

Fig. 9 Trimming overhangs of laminations accurately. The blank rides along block at point X, the saw blade is flush with this edge

Fig. 10 A table lamp completed by the methods described

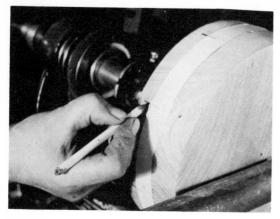

Fig. 11 If a piece of paper which exactly fits round the outside of the blank is folded the required number of times and marked at the folds, it can be used as shown to divide the work prior to drilling for the insertion of plugs

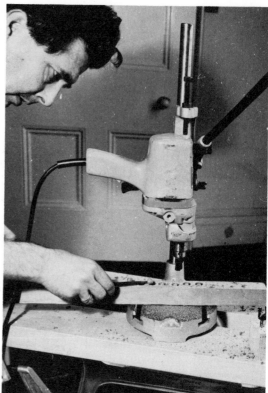

Fig. 13 Special cutter being used to cut plugs for insertion into the perimeter of a bowl blank

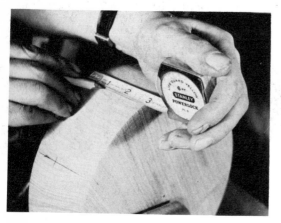

Fig. 12 (*left*) Using a rule to mark the exact positions before drilling

Inlaying is simple and effective. A groove or grooves can be cut round the bowl with a sharp parting tool, and the thin inlay strips, which have been prepared on the sawbench, can be steamed or wetted if necessary before they are glued in place. They should be left a little proud, as with the plugs, so that they can be trimmed flush when set. They can be held in place while drying by string, or adhesive tape. Plugs or inlays in the lid of a bowl look very nice, but be careful or a good bowl may be spoiled.

One aspect of built-up work which has a great appeal is the chequered bowl, made up of numbers of small wooden bricks. The beginner tends to fight shy of this sort of thing, which looks too difficult, but with care it is easy to do, and very good results can be had. The principle can be applied to other things beside bowls, such as biscuit barrels and vases. Making bowls in this way offers some advantages which offset the time spent in making the blanks. There is no need to bandsaw a disc, no hollowing as such to be done,

Fig. 14 Using a planer with thicknesser to prepare material for laminated work. Planer shown has power-fed thicknesser

Fig. 16 (*right*) Using a home-made jig to produce bricks with a set angle. The construction of this jig must be extremely accurate

Fig. 15 A cramp, such as the *Flexicramp*, is useful for clamping bowls built up by the brick method

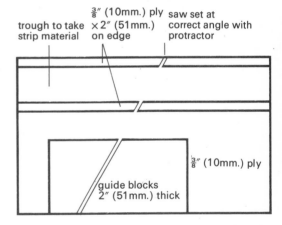

little waste of wood, and no problems with end grain, because the grain runs round the blank. Because of the latter fact, the whole turning operation can be done with a sharp scraper if you so desire, but a sharp gouge properly applied will do the job faster and cleaner. It saves time to make up a number of these blanks, and I usually have a day at it once I start.

If you have a planer with thicknessing attachment, the preparation of the material will be easy, Fig. 14. If not you should be able to get ready-thicknessed strips of contrasting wood from good timber

suppliers, but remember that it is vital for each brick in any one ring to be exactly the same thickness. If there is any variation, there will be bad joints, which can be dangerous.

One of the best ways of cramping such assemblies is with a special cramp, Fig. 15, which is designed for the job, and will increase the safety factor considerably. These are regularly advertised in the woodworking press, and can probably be obtained from the bigger tool stores. Even and strong pressure is exerted by these cramps, and I do not recommend home-made devices.

Fig. 17

Fig. 18 (above)

Fig. 19 (below)

If these blanks are properly made, and the lathe run at a sensible speed, the turning is not dangerous. Bases for such bowls should be made from plywood rather than natural timber, since the latter is likely to move with changes of humidity, and if this occurs, the bowl will be ruined. The angle for cutting the bricks is arrived at in the same way as for the segments, once the number of bricks in each ring has been decided on. The cutting of the bricks must be done with the utmost precision, for the slightest error will mean gaps in the assembly. The cutting can be done on a sawbench, using a mitre gauge, or a jig made up for the purpose, Fig. 16. If such a jig is used, the success of the whole operation will depend upon the accuracy of its construction, so it must be tried out on scrap material and adjusted until the results are perfect.

The blocks could be cut by hand in a mitre box with a slot cut in it at the required angle, but this is a slow and probably less accurate way. A stop of some kind would be needed to ensure that each block was the same length, and this would need a rebate in the lower surface, to prevent sawdust from affecting the accuracy. It you are fortunate enough to possess a radial arm saw such as the De Walt, the angle cutting is a simple matter. The blocks which form the bottom of the assembly are cut from wider stock than the rest, Fig. 17, so that they can be blended into the base of the bowl, which must be done with care on a ply base if it is not to look ugly. It is better to put these wider blocks in last, so that the assembly is upside down, which will allow excess glue to drain out of it rather than in.

If you are going to leave the blank in the cramp until the glue has set, your production will be halted,

Fig. 17 Turning a bowl built up in brick form, here the bottom layer of bricks is being blended into the plywood base

Fig. 18 Building up the bricks inside the cramp. It is sometimes necessary to tap the last one in each ring into place

Fig. 19 Turning the outside of a brick-formed bowl using a sharp scraper inclined down. Since the grain of the assembly runs round the blank, there will be no trouble with end grain

but this can be overcome by making a number of simple wooden cramping jigs, which are just two circles of stout ply with a bolt through the middle, Fig. 20. If one of these is applied to the build-up at this stage, with some paper interposed to prevent permanent adhesion between jig and work, it can be tightened up, and the cramp removed to start the next assembly, Fig. 21.

When making up these blanks it is vital to see that the surface on which you work is absolutely flat, and I keep a disc of aluminium for the purpose. The bowl bases are cut from thick plywood, a little smaller than the diameter of the blank, to save unnecessary turning, since ply is notorious for taking the edge off tools. The easiest way to centre them to the blank is to put some small blocks round the edge, and once they are in place, a heavy weight can be put on until they have dried. Many patterns are possible, and it is a good idea to experiment with some dry assemblies until you find what you want.

The turning itself is pleasant, and the beginner should use a scraper. Light cutting is needed, and digs must be avoided at all costs. The cutting edges will be dulled more rapidly than usual, so they must be given a rub from time to time. In the polishing and sanding of built-up work, it should be borne in mind that some adhesives may be softened by heat, and quite a lot can be generated by friction during these processes.

The depth of this sort of cramp will be sufficient for normal purposes, but you can glue two assemblies together if you wish to make a really deep blank.

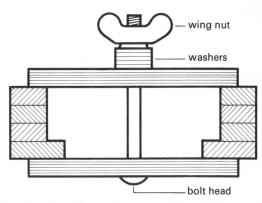

Fig. 20 Two pieces of stout ply with a bolt through the centre can be used to cramp up the assemblies. The cramp can then be removed and used again

Fig. 21 Built-up assembly cramped in a vice between two pieces of ply while the glue sets

Chapter ten

The production of objects such as vases and tankards by coopering methods is interesting, but it calls for just as much care and accuracy as any other form of built-up work, and it is not a field in which the slapdash worker is likely to succeed. The angles must be exact, and the assembly done with care, but apart from this it is easy.

Deep objects turned from the solid can take a long time to hollow out, as we discovered with the tea caddy. It is a laborious and tricky task, so something which is already hollow is worth considering. There is also the fact that when hollowing is done from the solid a lot of good timber is wasted, so the time taken in making the coopered blanks will be well repaid. If the angles in this sort of work are right, then they are near enough, but if they are near enough, they are not right! Use a hollow ground sawblade to get smooth edges, and do not sand them after cutting. I use epoxy resin glues on this sort of work, and I pay special attention to the cramping. The blanks should be left under pressure in a warm room until the glue has cured properly Fig. 1, preferably for two days.

For the sake of convenience the blanks are made up about 18in. or 2ft. (457·2mm. or 609·6mm.) long, and cut to the desired lengths afterwards, and here again the bandsaw proves its worth, Fig. 2. You can taper the staves slightly if you wish, so that the blank itself is tapered, and the small blanks after cutting will vary in size, and can be made up into sets. The staves are ripped up on the sawtable Fig. 3, the angle of tilt being found by dividing the number of staves into 180 and subtracting the result from 90. There are no doubt other ways, but that is how I do it. In work as critical as this it is better not to rely too much on the graduated scale on the sawbench, but to make up an accurate template in ply or hardboard, and use this to set the table. Large hose clips will do for cramps, or on the tapered blanks metal or wooden rings can be driven on to hold the staves in close contact. Do see to it that enough pressure is applied, because work of this nature could cause serious injury if it were to break up in the lathe, although such an eventuality is unlikely with today's adhesives.

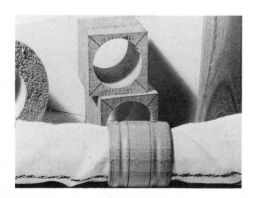

Serviette rings, still much in demand, are easily made with the items shown here.

Fig. 1 A coopered assembly under tourniquet tension

Fig. 2 The tubular assembly being cut to length on the bandsaw

To taper the staves on the sawbench you can make up one of the jigs shown in Fig. 4, the wood is put in, and jig and work ride along the fence together, Fig. 5. For our purposes a taper of about $\frac{1}{2}$in. to $\frac{5}{8}$in. (12·7mm. to 15·9mm.) on a stave of 18in. (457·2mm.) will be sufficient, and this is so slight that it can all be cut from one side.

When the tubular blanks have been made up, they are cut to length on the bandsaw, Fig. 6, and it will help with the tapered ones if the smaller end is packed up with scrap wood so that the cut ends will be square. Now you can make a tapered wooden mandrel from a piece of scrap, and drive the blank on to this firmly. This is mounted between centres and a rebate is cut to take the base, Fig. 7 and 8. The fitting of the base is important, and must be done carefully, because the blank will be mounted by this on a woodscrew chuck for the rest of the turning. After the rebate has been cut the bottom is turned up on a woodscrew chuck from a suitable piece of hardwood, a little larger than the base of the blank, and itself rebated to be an exact fit, Fig. 9 and 10.

Once the bottom has been fitted and allowed to dry, the assembly is mounted on the large wood-screw chuck, Fig. 11, and the inside is shaped, Fig. 12, using a sharp round-nosed scraper, and

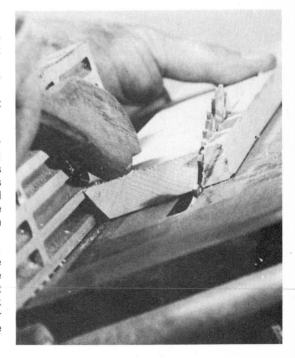

Fig. 3 Bevel ripping the staves for coopered blanks, on a sawtable which has been tilted to the required angle. A push stick must be used, and the guard has been removed purely for clarity

Fig. 4 (above)

Fig. 5 (below)　Fig. 7 (above)

Fig. 8 (below)

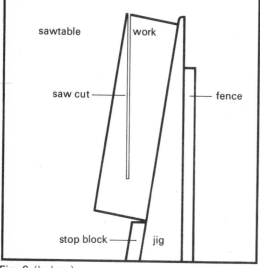

sawtable　work

saw cut —　　　　　— fence

stop block —　　jig

Fig. 6 (below)

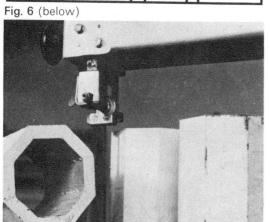

Fig. 4 Tapering jig in use on the circular saw

Fig. 5 Simple jig for cutting taper on a sawbench.
Jig and work slide together along fence

Fig. 6 One blank has been cut into three pieces on
the bandsaw to form three separate articles

Fig. 7 One blank has been driven on to a tapered
mandrel turned up on a woodscrew chuck. The
tool rest is placed across the face of the work so
that a rebate can be cut to take the base

Fig. 8 Showing the rebate cut in the end of the
blank ready for fitting the bottom

Fig. 10

Fig. 11
Fig. 12

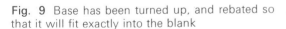

Fig. 9

Fig. 9 Base has been turned up, and rebated so that it will fit exactly into the blank

Fig. 10 Glue has been run round the rebate in the blank, and the base will now be fitted and subjected to pressure while drying

Fig. 11 Assembly mounted on large woodscrew chuck ready for turning

Fig. 12 Shaping the inside, using the round-nosed scraper

taking very light cuts. Any attempt to hurry, or to cut heavily, is likely to have the job off the chuck. When the inside is finished, it can be sanded, and a tapered plug fitted to the mouth so that the tailstock can be brought up to support the job. Now the outside can be shaped, Fig. 13, with a sharp gouge, well over on its side, and remember to keep that bevel rubbing. You can make blanks of this kind in one wood, with spacers, Fig. 14, or in contrasting woods, Fig. 15.

Fig. 13 Shaping the outside of the blank, using a sharp ¾in. [10·1mm.] roughing gouge, with light cuts. A tapered plug could be inserted in the end and tailstock support given if required

Drinking tankards can be made in oak, the handle being cut out and sanded, then fixed in position with glue and small brass screws through from the inside. You can fume these to give them a look of age if you wish, by suspending them in a tea chest or similar box, with a saucer of full strength ammonia in the bottom. Cover the top, and leave them until they have turned the requisite colour. Some examples of this tankard work are done by preparing the blank very carefully so that it is possible to leave the inside unturned, which is attractive, and saves time.

It appears that everyone who takes an interest in woodturning sooner or later wants to make serviette rings. It is a fiddly business, and I avoid it whenever I can, but there is some merit in it, in that very little wood is required, and there seems to be a ready sale for such things. They can be made either from solid wood, or from laminated blanks, but if you choose the latter method you must be extremely careful about centring the blocks, otherwise the pattern will be ruined. It is possible to bore the hole after doing the turning, but a great deal easier if the boring is done first. The size of the blocks used is a matter of taste to some extent, but a two inch cube will do for a start.

Fig. 14 A coopered blank made with tempered hardboard spacers

The hole should be about 1½in. (38·1mm.) in diameter, and can be drilled on a drill press, or by the method I am using in Fig. 17 and 18, feeding the wood to a cutter in the headstock by means of the mortiser. You could simply use the tailstock to feed the wood to the cutter, but then it would be best to go through about halfway and reverse the block. The tailstock centre is removed, and a piece of scrap can be used as a pressure pad.

Fig. 15

Fig. 16

Fig. 17 (above)　　　　　　　　　　Fig. 18 (below)

Fig. 15 Small plant pot holder made in contrasting woods

Fig. 16 Before and after. The finished turning on the left could be fitted with a handle to form a tankard. It could also be used as a vase

Fig. 17 Drilling a hole through a square blank in preparation for turning a serviette ring. In this case the work is held on a mortising attachment, and the drill held in a chuck on the mandrel

Fig. 18 The drilling of the hole requires a low speed on the lathe, achieved in this case by the use of the gearbox, and the shavings should be as shown here

The next job will be to turn up a tapered wooden mandrel, Fig. 19, so that the blanks can be tapped into position on it, Fig. 20, and held while the outside is turned, Fig. 21. Use light cuts, and when you are satisfied, the outside can be sanded and polished. The length of the mandrel is not critical, but make it long enough to give you room to work —say 8in. (203·2mm.) or so.

When the outside is finished, the blank is removed from the mandrel so that the inside can be dealt with. It is possible to do this by hand, but much more satisfactory to make a hollow chuck from a piece of softwood, so that it just accepts the ring as an interference fit, Fig. 22. Hardwood can be used, but softwood has a bit more give in it, and so is often better for jobs of this nature. Trim up the inside of the hole with a sharp scraper, inclined down, and bell out the edges of the hole slightly, then sand and polish. Obviously one does not go through all this for each ring, it is better to have two or three dozen blanks, taking them all through each stage before going on to the next. Since serviette rings normally go in sets, careful use of calipers and dividers will be needed to get a true match.

The use of tapered mandrels and hollow chucks is by no means confined to the production of serviette rings, similar methods are used in making salt and pepper pots, wooden rings, circular picture frames, and what have you. Many turners enjoy making cruets, and little blue glass liners for the mustard pots can be purchased. Sets like this look well on wooden trays, and they are easy to make if you go about the job correctly. Articles which have holes, like salt and pepper pots, should always be drilled before turning, because if they are turned first it is very unlikely that it will be possible to drill a truly central hole. Blocks for cruets are first prepared to length and drilled to the desired depth with a drill about one inch wide. In the case of the mustard pot, the hole should be drilled to accept the liner as a free fit, but in the absence of a large enough drill the hole should be made as wide as possible, and opened out afterwards with a parting tool.

Taking the salt and pepper pots first, there are two ways of tackling the shaping of the outside. The block can be mounted between centres, with a plug of wood in the hole to support the tailstock

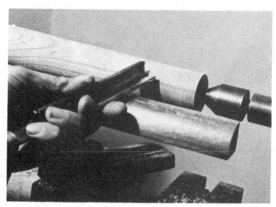

Fig. 19

Fig. 20

Fig. 21

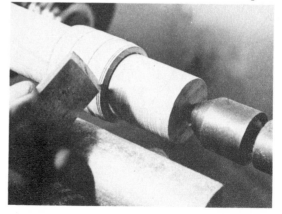

Fig. 22

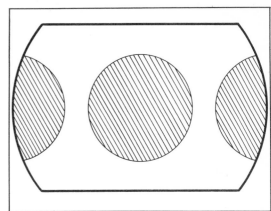

Fig. 23

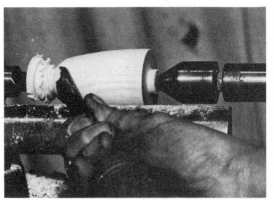

Fig. 24

Fig. 25

Fig. 19 Turning up a tapered wooden mandrel to take the blanks for the serviette rings as a drive fit

Fig. 20 A blank tapped into position on the tapered mandrel, and the tool rest positioned for turning

Fig. 21 Turning the outside of the serviette ring, and decorating with incised lines

Fig. 22 After the outside has been turned, the blank is put in a hollow softwood chuck, so that the inside can be cleaned up, and a slight chamfer put on the inner edges

Fig. 23 Post blocked serviette ring. Many designs are possible

Fig. 24 Shaping the outside of a salt or pepper pot, after the block has been pre-drilled, and a small plug inserted in the hole, so that the tailstock centre can be used. If a revolving centre is used, there may be no need for a wooden plug

Fig. 25 Turning a mustard pot on a woodscrew chuck. Note glass lines being tried for fit

centre if necessary, and the job treated as a normal piece of spindle turning, Fig. 24. An alternative is to turn up a slightly tapered plug chuck, and drive the block on to this. Cutting is done with a sharp gouge, but do not cut too heavily, or the blank may move on the plug. If the former method is adopted, the blank should be left a little longer than the intended height, so that a waste piece can be left at the headstock end, this being cut off afterwards. When sanding and polishing have been completed, the small holes can be drilled in the tops, and plugs fitted to the bases. Special plastic ones can be bought, or corks can be used. The mustard pot is a simple turning operation, both pot and lid being turned on a woodscrew chuck, Figs. 25 to 26. When the lid has been made and polished it can be parted off.

Wooden rings, and circular picture frames, are made in a similar manner. The blank is turned to exact size on a woodscrew chuck, and its outer edge shaped, Fig. 27, after which it is driven into a hollow chuck made from softwood, and having a slight taper on its inner surface. The finish on this surface is left rough to give a better grip. The inside diameter is now marked, and a cut made inside the line into the waste, using the parting tool and going about half way through the wood, Fig. 28. The ring is then shaped with a $\frac{3}{8}$in. (9·5mm.) gouge, on its side, and taking off a clean shaving, Fig. 29. Sand this side, reverse the job in the chuck, and complete the ring by repeating the process, but go carefully as you cut through the wood, Fig. 30. If you are making a circular picture frame, the first part of the job will be the same as for the

Fig. 26 Lid of mustard pot being turned from a block on woodscrew chuck

Fig. 27 Shaping the outer edge of a disc which is to be made into a ring

ring, the face of the frame being shaped and polished. When the blank is reversed it is marked out, the rebate for the glass cut with a parting tool, and the waste cut away.

Those who have watched professional turners at exhibitions making egg cups, will appreciate that something attractive and useful can be made in a few minutes from a mere scrap of wood, and it may be because of this that beginners are so keen to make them. Unfortunately, however, some very odd things have been written about the making of egg cups, some of which can scarcely lead to anything but frustration, unless the turner is very highly skilled—in which case he is hardly likely to pay any attention to them. It has, for example,

been suggested that they be turned up in 'sticks', several at a time. I would say that if the student tries this once, he is unlikely to repeat the experiment, and he will be a wiser man for his trouble. I say this for two reasons, one being that if the egg cups are shaped before they are hollowed they will whip under pressure from the hollowing tool, and may even snap at the stem. Apart from this, once the cups have been parted off from the stick, the problem of mounting them in the lathe so that they will run true, whilst perhaps not insurmountable, will call for a high degree of skill and ingenuity. There is a queer sort of device for turning egg cups and the like, which used to be on sale at one time, and I had one made, Fig. 31, but I do not like it at all.

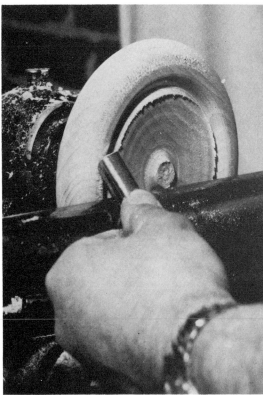

Fig. 28 Forming the ring by cutting in with a parting tool, the work will be reversed into a hollow chuck

Fig. 29 Shaping the ring, with a ⅜in. [9·5mm.] gouge on its side

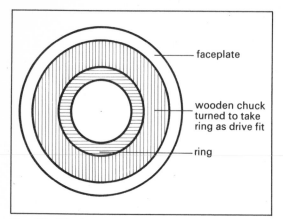

Fig. 30 Blank reversed in chuck, and now cut through

Labels in diagram: faceplate; wooden chuck turned to take ring as drive fit; ring

Fig. 31 Special chuck which can be made easily by a metal worker for holding blanks for egg cups. These must first be turned to a cylinder with a flange at the bottom to fit the flange in the chuck

Another idea which is sometimes put forward, I suspect by people who have not tried it, is that the block be mounted on a woodscrew chuck and hollowed out by feeding a home-made spade-shaped cutter into it, this being held in the tail-stock. Try this, by all means, it sometimes works, but it has little to do with being a woodturner. Anyone who has taken the trouble to master the technique of hollowing egg cups with a sharp $\frac{1}{4}$in. (6·4mm.) gouge will be able to perform the operation quicker than any gimmick. There are a number of undesirable practices which one sees recommended on occasions, which have no connection with craftsmanship, such as the use of a woodworker's plane to smooth spindle work, supported on tool rests. This may be of help to the man who is incapable of using a skew chisel properly, but craftsmen do not need makeshift methods.

If you turn egg cups by the means described here you will not have much trouble, all you want is patience and plenty of practice. The shape I am dealing with now is the one I use for exhibition work, because it incorporates most of the basic cuts, and if the hollowing technique is mastered it will be found useful in other jobs. Practice in making egg cups in sets, with a really accurate match, will help a lot when other types of copy work have to be done.

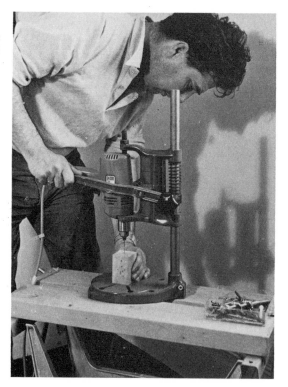

Fig. 32 Pre-drilling with a $\frac{1}{16}$in. [1·6mm.] drill on egg cup blocks

Fig. 33

Fig. 34

Egg cups are turned on the smaller of the wood-screw chucks because the base of this does not obstruct the cutting tools. The novice may be a little apprehensive about the holding power of a single screw in end grain. But if the tools are sharp and the cuts light, all will be well. A hardwood such as beech, elm, or utile should be used, though I have turned egg cups in pine on a single screw. The blocks used should be a full 2in. (50·8mm.) square and about 3in. (76·2mm.) long, or just under, and the ends must be cut off at right angles or they will not run true on the chuck, and so some of the diameter will be lost.

Fig. 35

Fig. 36

Fig. 33 Rough block prior to reducing to a cylinder with roughing gouge

Fig. 34 The end of the block, which has now been turned to a cylinder, is faced off and made slightly concave, using a parting tool. A cleaner finish would be obtained by using the point of a skew, but with a cutting, rather than a scraping action

Fig. 35 Corner of skew being used to clean up concave face of block

Fig. 36 The centre of the block is found by holding a bradawl on the tool rest at about 45° to the work. When the exact centre has been found, the bradawl is pushed in to guide the screw when the block is reversed

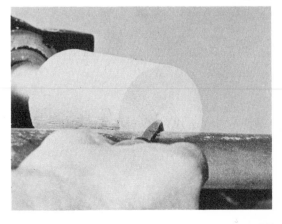

The ends are marked by drawing in the diagonals to find the centre, in the usual way, and a bradawl pushed in to give a start for the screw. If you are going to make quite a number of egg cups it is better to prepare the blocks first, then pre-drill in a drill press, using a $\frac{1}{16}$th (1·6mm.) drill, Fig. 32. The woodscrew chuck can now be firmly attached to the mandrel, and the block mounted. Screw it on firmly, but beware of overdoing it or you may have trouble. With the wood mounted, the tool rest is brought into place, Fig. 33, and the square block taken down to a cylinder with the roughing gouge in the manner described earlier. If you wish, you can bring up the tailstock during this part of the job, to give a little extra support.

It will not matter if you do not bring the wood quite to a cylinder at this stage, but when it is more or less round, the end can be faced off and made slightly concave, Fig. 34. You can do this with a parting tool, but the finish will be rough, and the corner of a sharp skew will make a better job, Fig. 35. Remember to use only the point, leaning the rest of the blade just a fraction away from the wood. Now the tool rest is brought round so that it is across the end of the block, and the centre is marked while the wood is revolving using the point of a bradawl held on the tool rest at an angle of about 45° to the work, Fig. 36. When the exact centre has been found, the bradawl is pushed straight into the work for $\frac{1}{2}$in. (12·7mm.) or so, the lathe is stopped, and the work reversed on the chuck. Because the base has been made concave, there will now be line contact with the edge of the chuck, giving a firm mounting, and the cup, when finished, will stand without rocking. After this the tool rest is returned to its original position along the work, and a light cut or two taken with a sharp gouge, to correct any inaccuracy in the remounting.

At this point you can either go ahead and make the first egg cup of the set freehand, subsequently using it as a master for the remaining ones, or a setting out board can be made as in Fig. 37. This is simply a small piece of scrap wood on which are marked the height of the foot, length of the stem, amount of radius on bottom of cup, and exact overall height. The accepted way with these little marking boards is to make pencil marks at the appropriate points, then push the edge of a chisel in to make small vee cuts which will guide the

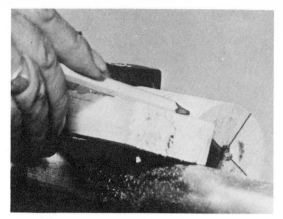

Fig. 37

Fig. 38

Fig. 39

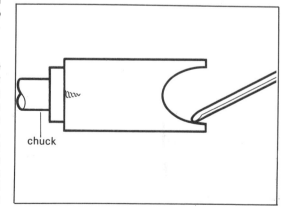

chuck

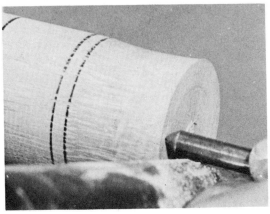

Fig. 40

Fig. 41

pencil. If you like you can make a board with small pointed nails in its edge, so that you can place it flat on the tool rest and push it against the wood, thus marking it clearly. If this is done, the tool rest must be close to the work, for safety's sake.

When the marking out has been completed, any excess wood beyond the length mark can be cut away with the parting tool, Fig. 38, and the concave shape of the outside of the cup formed with a sharp gouge or skew chisel. At this juncture the blank

Fig. 37 A setting out board with the salient points marked along its edge is used to mark out the work after reversing on the chuck

Fig. 38 Excess wood beyond the height mark on the block is cut away with the parting tool

Fig. 39 Hollowing egg cup blank with small gouge. The tool is working against the grain, but final cuts with a sharp scraper from inside outwards will smooth the surface

Fig. 40 Commencement of hollowing cut on an egg cup, using a spindle gouge with a fairly short bevel. It is at right angles to the tool rest, and on its side

Fig. 41 Continuation of hollowing cut on egg cup block. As the tool moves in towards the centre, it is rolled half on to its back

should be hollowed, while it still has plenty of strength. If the outside shaping is done before the hollowing there may be troubles due to judder caused by flexing of the stem, and possible fracture of the stem itself.

As far as the hollowing is concerned, the principle is most important. Small items of this sort, where the tools are working on end grain, can be excavated with scrapers with reasonable results, though the method is slow, and a sharp gouge is considerably more efficient. I realise that I am preaching against myself here, for you can see from the sketch Fig. 39 that the gouge will be cutting against the grain, which is unlikely unless the gouge is blunt, the final cuts can be made with the grain, using a round-nosed scraper from the centre outwards, which will improve matters.

Now let us examine the exact method of hollowing out an article of this nature with the $\frac{1}{4}$in. (6·4mm.) spindle gouge. It will help if the bevel on this is rather shorter than would normally be used on spindle work, since we want a rounded end rather than a pointed one which may catch in the wood. The tool rest is positioned across the end of the work, close to it, and a little below centre, the cutting being done from the outside inwards. If it was started at the centre, working gradually outwards, there would be trouble with the gouge skidding at the start of each successive cut, since there would be no support for the bevel until the cut was under way. The action is a scooping one, beginning with the gouge completely on its side, and square to the tool rest, Fig. 40, lowering the handle and rolling the tool half on to its back as the cut proceeds, Fig. 41. This may seem awkward at first, but the illustrations will make it clear, and one soon acquires the knack. If a scraper is used to finish off, a sweeping action is required, keeping the tool flat on the rest, and pivoting it between this and the thumb to get a smooth curve. Cut from the centre outwards, and lightly. Too thin an edge on the cup should be avoided, since it will be weak, and if really thin it could cause an injury to the hand during the sanding or polishing.

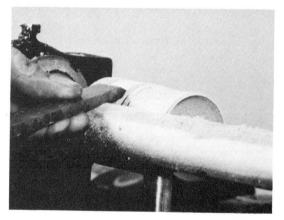

When the inside is completed, work can commence on the shaping of the egg cup. The reason for hollowing first will now be apparent, since with the walls as thin as they are, cutting on them would be difficult. Set the tool rest along the work, rather low, as the parting tool will be used next, and it cuts a lot better when pointing upwards. We are going to rough out the shape of the stem, so a cut is made just to the right of the line which marks the foot, and another just to the left of the one marking the bottom of the cup, going in to leave about $\frac{3}{4}$in. (19·1mm.) of wood, Fig. 42. If the exact size required here is known, calipers can be used, and the wood left $\frac{1}{16}$in. (1·6mm.) oversize to allow for finishing.

The remainder of the waste can be taken out with the parting tool, but the accepted way is with a chisel. I mentioned this when we were discussing the removal of wood from between sizing cuts, but it is worth stressing because it is such a very useful cut. Set the tool rest almost level with the top of the work, and have the chisel as sharp as possible. The tool goes dead flat on the rest, with its cutting

Fig. 42

Fig. 43
Fig. 44

Fig. 42 Two cuts are made with the parting tool to form the base and cup portions

Fig. 43 The tool rest has been raised, and a sharp skew chisel is used to take out the waste wood between the parting tool cuts

Fig. 44 $\frac{1}{2}$in. [12·7mm.] shallow spindle gouge being used to shape the foot of the egg cup. Note that the bevel is rubbing

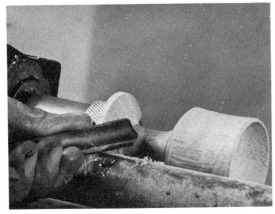

Fig. 45

Fig. 46

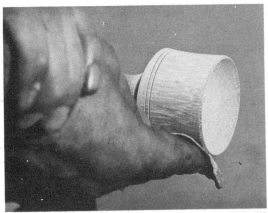

Fig. 47
Fig. 48

edge parallel to the axis of the job. Place it on the work so that it is too far forward to cut, and draw it back until the cut begins. Now take the edge forward and down in an arc, and you should have one of those lovely long shavings we hear so much about! Once you have the knack of this technique I think you will enjoy using it, Fig. 43.

When this part of the job is completed, a little shaping can be done on the foot, and to the radius on the bottom of the cup, using the point of a skew or a sharp gouge, Fig. 44. Sometimes when the bottom of the cup is shaped, some ribbing marks may appear, due to whip in the stem, and the answer is to steady the cup with one hand as these cuts are made, or if really necessary bring up the tailstock for a moment.

The concave shape of the stem is now put in with a sharp gouge, Fig. 45, and the little shoulders at

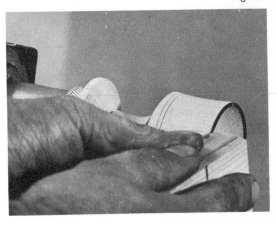

Fig. 45 $\frac{1}{2}$in. [12·7mm.] shallow spindle gouge being used to shape the stem

Fig. 46 Forming the small shoulders at each end of the stem, with the long corner of a skew chisel

Fig. 47 Sanding the outside of the egg cup. Note that one hand supports the other, and the abrasive paper is held under the work

Fig. 48 Blackening the edge by frictional pressure from scrap wood

each end can be cut in with the point of a chisel, Fig. 46. The two little incised lines round the bottom of the cup are put in with the skew point, and the turning part of the job is over.

The cup can now be sanded inside and out, Fig. 47 but if you have been turning properly there should be no need for much of this. Some like to burn the edge of the cup by pressing a scrap of wood against it while it is revolving, Fig. 48, but watch your fingers! This is said to strengthen the edge, rather as wooden spear points were hardened in the fire, but whether it does or not, it is an attractive finishing touch, Fig. 49 and 50.

A set of egg cups all alike is not a difficult project. You need measuring devices, such as dividers and calipers, and plenty of patience. Such sets need a tray or stand, and this makes a nice little combined spindle and faceplate exercise. A circular tray can be turned up on the larger of the woodscrew chucks, with its edge neatly shaped, and the tray hollowed with the aid of a bowl gouge, parting tool, and scraper.

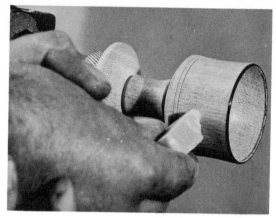

Fig. 49

A disc of wood of suitable size for the number of cups in the set, and about $\frac{3}{4}$in. (19·1mm.) thick, is mounted on the chuck, and its face made slightly concave, using the gouge well over on its side. The tool rest will be well below centre for this, and close to the work, 51. This surface will be the bottom of the tray, so it can be sanded, the centre marked, and the disc reversed on the chuck. When this has been done, a small sharp gouge is used to shape the edge, care being taken to see that no roughness is left on the end grain. This is important, and if it is present it must be dealt with as in Chapter Eight on bowl work, with a small and very sharp gouge cutting lightly, Fig. 52. The hollowing out of the tray is a simple enough matter, we use a parting tool to start the job, beginning near the edge and leaving the required thickness of wall, Fig. 53. The job can be completed in this manner, but the student should by now be proficient with the gouge, which will make a faster job of it, Fig. 54

Final trimming of flat surfaces like this one is done with a sharp scraper, shaped square across the end, and having its corners radiused a little so that they do not score the work, Fig. 55. This will give a true flat bottom to the tray, which is most important,

Fig. 50
Fig. 51

Fig. 52

Fig. 55

Fig. 53
Fig. 54

Fig. 49 Carnauba wax applied to the outside of the egg cup, which has previously been burnished with shavings

Fig. 50 Correct pressure with a soft rag will now bring the work to a brilliant gloss

Fig. 51 Cleaning up an oak disc cut from an old table top to make a tray for the egg cup set

Fig. 52 Trueing up the outer edge of the disc with a small gouge

Fig. 53 Commencing the hollowing of the tray using a sharp parting tool, handle well down

Fig. 54 A bowl gouge will give a quicker and cleaner finish

Fig. 55 Square scraper with corners radiused, used to get a flat surface in the bottom of the tray

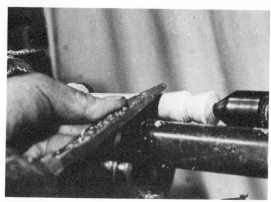

Fig. 56

Fig. 59

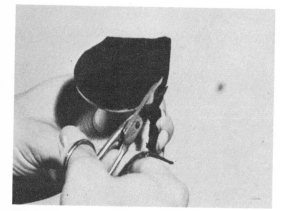

Fig. 57

Fig. 58

Fig. 56 Turning the handle of the tray between centres

Fig. 57 Self-adhesive green baize applied to the bottoms of the cups and trimmed back with sharp scissors will give a neat and effective finish

Fig. 58 A rectangular tray can be made, and the recesses for the bases of the egg cups made with a special cutter

Fig. 59 Close-up of the cutter used for the recesses. This must be made by a qualified worker or the egg cups will rock about instead of standing firmly. The wood at the centre, around the screw of the chuck, is not removed, but shaped so that the base of the handle can be blended into it. The latter is a simple spindle turning, and one's fancy can be given free rein with regard to shape, but it should not be made too ornate. Turn it up from a piece of wood about $\frac{3}{4}$in. (19·1mm.) square, a little longer than the intended length of the handle, so that a small waste piece can be left at each end, and parted off afterwards, Fig. 56. Once the tray is finished, the handle can be fitted, using a spot of glue, and a screw through from underneath. Do make sure that the handle is central, and truly vertical, or it will look bad. Some self-adhesive green baize can be applied to the bottom of the tray, and to the bases of the cups as well if you like, but cut this oversize, apply it, and then trim it back, Fig. 57, or it will go out of shape.

An alternative type of tray can be made in the form of a rectangular piece of wood, with the edges chamfered, and shallow recesses cut out to accept the bottoms of the cups. The cutting of these recesses must be done neatly, or the job will be spoiled, and a good method is shown in Fig. 58. The wood is carefully marked out to give the positions of the centres of the recesses, and mounted in the mortising attachment of the lathe, the depth stop of which is carefully set. The cutting is done with a small tool made from oddments of tool steel, Fig. 59, running the lathe, at its highest speed, and feeding the work to the cutter by means of the lever as in ordinary mortising. This job could be done on a drill press, using a high speed drill. Such cutters work well, but do have them made up by a qualified man, as a badly welded one could break and cause an injury.

Chapter eleven

Spiral work is interesting and attractive, but it is not strictly woodturning. It is relevant here, however, because the wood has to be prepared in a lathe, and the lathe is the obvious means of holding it while the marking out, and the somewhat tedious hand work are done. There are solid and hollow spirals, with varying numbers of twists, which look impressive, but are in reality very easy to make, requiring simply basic knowledge and patience. Candlesticks made in this way can be beautiful, but their manufacture is a matter of interest and a labour of love, they are not an economical proposition from a commercial viewpoint as far as the home worker is concerned.

The first step is to turn the blank itself to a cylinder of suitable size, and to mark on it the points at which the spiral is to start and finish. The section which is to form the spiral is now divided into equal parts, having a length roughly the same as the diameter of the wood, these divisions being made with heavy black lines, Fig. 1. Now divide these sections into quarters, Fig. 2, and then draw four lines along the whole spiral section, thus quartering it lengthwise, Fig. 3. This can be arrived at by measurement, but if you have used a four-pronged driving centre, lines drawn accurately through the marks left by this will enable you to mark the work, and the tool rest can be used as a ruler when the lines are drawn.

It will be appreciated that what we are making here can be compared to the thread of a screw, therefore the construction must take into account the question of pitch and lead. For those unfamiliar with these terms, pitch is the distance between the centres of adjacent ridges, and lead is the name for the distance travelled by our 'thread' in one complete revolution. Since we are at the moment making a single spiral, these happen to be the same, but in a double spiral the lead is twice the pitch, and in a triple it is three times. Starting at the left hand end of our marked area, the spiral is drawn in by sketching diagonally across the small divisions. If any difficulty is experienced here, some adhesive tape can be wrapped round the work as a guide, Fig. 4. The line thus made indicates the position of the ridge, so a second line, preferably in a different colour to avoid confusion, is drawn in

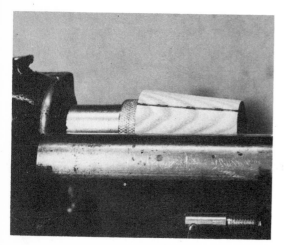

Tapered bobbin sander marked for cut with saw to hold ends of abrasive paper

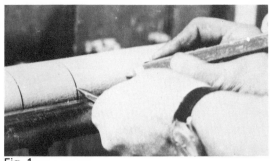

Fig. 1

Fig. 2

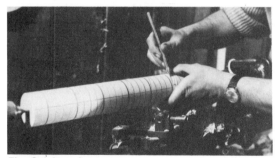

Fig. 3 (above)

Fig. 4 (below)

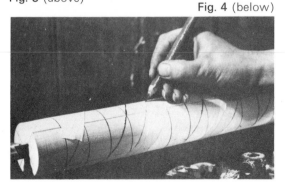

Fig. 5

to mark the position of the centre of the hollow. A cut is now made with a hand saw along this line to the required depth of the hollow, and to simplify this a piece of wood is clamped each side of the sawblade as a depth stop. From here on I regret to say that it is all a matter of slow, patient hand work. The hollow can be roughed out with a carving gouge and mallet, Fig. 5 and 6, and finished with Surform tools, rasps, and the like. Careful carving, filing, and sandpapering, will give a very attractive result, Fig. 7.

For a double twist, the preliminary marking out is as for the single, but this time the sections which give the pitch are divided into two parts instead of four. The ridge lines are marked as before, the two twists starting opposite each other. Again, lines are drawn in to indicate the centres of the hollows, and you cut to depth and finish off with carving tools.

Fig. 1 Dividing up the cylinder which is to be turned into a spiral into equal parts, the lengths being roughly that of the diameter

Fig. 2 The original divisions are now divided into four

Fig. 3 Four lines are drawn lengthwise on the blank, quartering it

Fig. 4 Marking out the ridge lines for the spiral, using adhesive tape as a guide

Fig. 5 Gouge and mallet being used to start roughing out the spiral

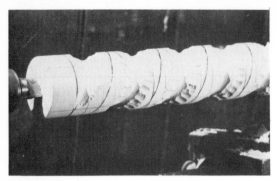

Fig. 6 The roughing out continues, but there is a lot left to do

Fig. 7 The spiral after a lot of work with rasps, files, etc

Fig. 8 Cutting a vee block to hold a cylindrical blank for drilling. Tool in use here is the De Walt radial arm saw

Hollow spirals are more impressive, these being made with two or more twists. The marking out for a double twist hollow spiral is as for the solid version, but the saw is not used. When the marking out has been done, the blank is placed in a vee block, Fig. 8, on the drill press, Fig. 9 (or mortiser, Fig. 10), centred to a drill of suitable size, and the roughing out completed by drilling through along the coloured lines so that the holes overlap, Fig. 11. A neater job may result if the drilling is not taken right through in one go, but done partly from each side, to avoid the wood breaking away as the drill comes through.

Tapered spirals can be made by tapering the blank, and adhering to the rule that the pitch is equal to the diameter; in other words, as the diameter decreases, the divisions become shorter, Fig. 15. First attempts in this sort of work should be done in a material which will not split too easily, yet be soft enough to carve and work. Beech would be a good choice, or a piece of cherry or sycamore. If you want to make candlesticks by these methods, it will be found easier to make the central, twisted part, as one unit. A pin can be turned at each end, and the top and base made separately and fitted later.

For lathes like my own Coronet one can purchase a wide variety of attachments, such as circular saws, planers, thicknessers, mortisers, and so on, which do not directly concern us here although they are useful. A bandsaw, as we have seen, is an invaluable item in the turner's shop, for the preparation of discs for every kind of faceplate work. Other attachments such as disc and belt sanders can be useful too, as can the three jawed chuck with tapered shank, Fig. 16. A beginner can buy far more than he really needs, however, and it is wisest at first to buy a good lathe and a set of decent quality tools, then settle down to learn the craft. Once some progress has been made, the individual will begin to see in which direction his interests lie, and so will not spend his money unwisely in making additions to his equipment. Most professional turners have a large number of tools, which they acquire over the years, but in their everyday work they use relatively few. There are jigs and fixtures which can be made at home to help in a number of lathe operations, but try not to become a slave to such things, or you will never really master the job properly.

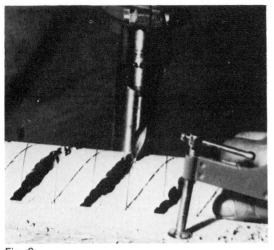

Fig. 9

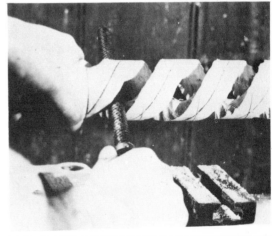

Fig. 12 (above)

Fig. 13 (below)

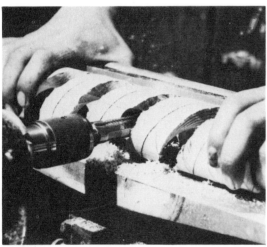

Fig. 10

Fig. 11

Fig. 9 Work being drilled through on a pillar drill whilst held in the vee block

Fig. 10 If you have a universal machine, the slot miller bit can be used, the work being fed to the cutter by the fence of the combination table

Fig. 11 The spiral begins to take shape. This job cannot be hurried

Fig. 12 A hand tool being used in the shaping

Fig. 13 Round rasp being used to get at the inside

Fig. 14

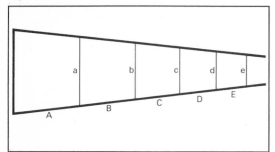

Fig. 15 (above)

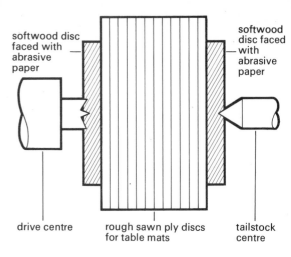

softwood disc faced with abrasive paper

softwood disc faced with abrasive paper

drive centre

rough sawn ply discs for table mats

tailstock centre

Fig. 17

Fig. 16 (below)

Various shapes in what are known as bobbin sanders can be made, and will be found useful. The sanding of fixed radii, as in the fitting of legs to the base of a tripod table is a good example of how these things can help. The abrasive paper can be stuck to these bobbins, but a better way is to make a sawcut lengthwise, tuck the ends of the paper into this, and wedge it with a scrap of softwood. This will facilitate the removal and replacement of the paper when it is worn out. You can buy loose abrasive granules, and bobbins which have concave or awkward contours can have this loose abrasive glued to them.

Fig. 14 A strip torn from an abrasive belt is used for the finishing

Fig. 15 In marking out for a tapered twist, the divisions decrease with the diameter. In the sketch above A =a, B =b, C =c, and so on

Fig. 16 Chuck with tapered shank being fitted to the mandrel

Fig. 17 Showing set-up for turning table mats

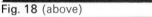
Fig. 18 (above) Fig. 19 (below)

Fig. 20

The turner may want to make such things as circular table mats, from plywood, which will have transfers applied, and be given a coat of varnish. Obviously you do not want a hole in the middle, so a disc of softwood is fixed to the faceplate, and the ply attached to it with a little glue, and some paper between to assist removal. In order to be sure of the mounting, the tailstock can be brought up, and a piece of scrap interposed between it and the work, Fig. 17. Some turners do not bother with glue at all, but stick some sandpaper to the face of the softwood to ensure a grip, and rely on firm tailstock pressure. The trimming to size and shape can be done with a gouge or a scraper, but the plywood soon spoils the edge of either. Toy wheels can be made in the same way, but the measuring must be very accurate.

Fig. 18 Turning a small cylindrical block to make buttons

Fig. 19 Shaping face of button on end of block

Fig. 20 Cutting in with chisel point to start formation of back

Wooden buttons for ladies' coats have always been expensive and here the turner will be able to display his skill without much trouble. A small block of wood is turned to the approximate diameter of the buttons needed, using the wood-screw chuck. The button is turned on the end of this, shaped, sanded, polished, and finally parted off, the back can be finished by hand, or a small hollow chuck can be made, as with the turning of a wooden ring, and the buttons finished in this, Figs. 18 to 22. The holes for the thread are marked carefully and drilled by hand.

Fig. 21 (above)

Fig. 22 (below)

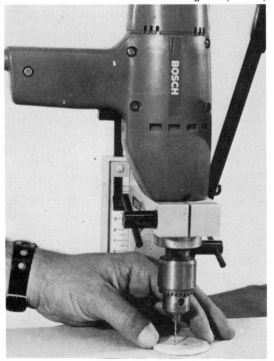

Fig. 21 Parting off when face has been sanded

Fig. 22 Drilling thread holes in button. Two holes are enough for a coat button.

Chapter twelve

This chapter is a mixed bag, in that it deals with the basic points in the making of lamps and tool handles; how to deal with long objects which can only be supported by the lathe itself at the driven end because they have to be bored or hollowed; and the construction of a pepper mill. I have also included details of one or two other chucks which can be made in the workshop, and are very useful.

Table lamps, bedside lamps, and the like, can be made entirely from the solid, Fig. 1, or in two parts, Fig. 2. The former method tends to be wasteful of wood, but saves time, and is a straightforward spindle turning operation. In the latter case, we have two separate turning jobs, one spindle for the stem of the lamp, and the other faceplate for the base, the two being joined after turning, Fig. 3.

This is done by turning a pin on the bottom of the lamp stem and a hole in the centre of the base, to accept the pin as a close fit. The depth of the hole needs to be just fractionally deeper than the length of the pin, but not too much, so that a gap-filling glue can be used to ensure strength. Two screws can be put through from the bottom if desired, to further strengthen the joint. If the base has sufficient thickness, it can be drilled through to take the flex, but if the shape does not permit this, a groove must be cut across the base, Fig. 4. The wire is glued into this with an epoxy resin glue, and a piece of green baize finishes it off.

In the making of pendant light fittings, the techniques already discussed are applicable, in particular the turning of spheres. Standard lamps are always popular, and a look round some of the bigger stores will soon convince you that they are worth making, since the prices asked are very high. The stem for these can best be made in two sections, joined with a pin and a hole, and matching the grain as well as possible. A bead, or other decorative device strategically placed will conceal the joint, Fig. 5. The base is a fairly big and heavy faceplate job, so keep the speed down. Three or

Fig. 1 Table lamps for children. These were turned from pine and sprayed with enamel, transfers being fixed after drying

Fig. 2 An oak table lamp made in two parts with a pin on the stem to fit the hole in the base

four small feet can be turned up on the woodscrew chuck for the base, in fact the little off-centred club foot would do well.

Wall light fittings are not only useful, but readily saleable if well made, and there is quite a bit of turning involved. Grooving for the wiring can best be done with a slot miller bit in the lathe, using the auxiliary table, Fig. 6.

The making of tool handles is traditional to the woodturner, who is hardly likely to go out and buy them! If you make your own, do see that they are long enough. The turning is no problem, a piece of

Fig. 3 A two-part table lamp completed

Fig. 4 A groove must be run in the bases of some lamps so that the wire can be glued into it before baize is fitted

1½in. (38·1mm.) square wood about 12in. to 14in. (304·8mm. to 355·6mm.) long, is put in the lathe, brought to a cylinder, and the whole of the shaping can be done with the roughing gouge, if you like. Finish with a smoothing cut from a sharp skew, and then a little fine sandpaper, or garnet. If a dead centre is used when turning tool handles, it will be possible to put the piece of copper or brass pipe which is to form the ferrule over this at the beginning, so that it can be tried for fit when the stepped piece is turned with the parting tool, Figs. 7 and 8. When the ferrule has finally been driven on, it can be polished up with a piece of emery cloth, and its edge smoothed with a scraper.

Now what about such things as really tall vases, maybe 12in. (304·8mm.) more in length, which have to be hollowed? The first move, as with any other vase blank, is to drill a hole to the required

---

Fig. 5 (*left*) Where the two parts of a standard lamp fit together, some form of decorative bead should be placed to conceal the joint

Fig. 6 (*below*) Grooving the arms of wall light fittings to take the wire. Alternatively, groove can be in upper surface

Fig. 7 Shaping the end of a tool handle for the fitting of brass or copper ferrule

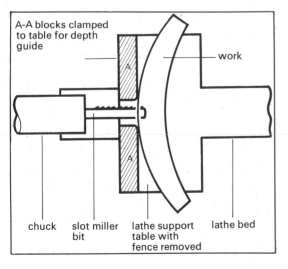

A-A blocks clamped to table for depth guide

work

chuck · slot miller bit · lathe support table with fence removed · lathe bed

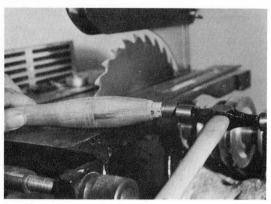

Fig. 8 Driving on the ferrule

Fig. 9 Preparing a blank for making a tall wooden vase

depth. The blank is then mounted between centres and run down to a cylinder, Fig. 9, after which a hollow wooden chuck is turned up, and the blank driven into it as a close fit.

Before we can proceed, it will be necessary to make up a wooden steady, Fig. 10, this being capable of adjustment to the diameter of the cylinder being worked. When this is ready, it is fitted to the lathe saddle, and the tailstock is brought up to align the job while the steady is fitted and adjusted. A little wax rubbed on at the point where the steady rubs will save burning the wood. Once the steady has been set up, the tailstock can be removed, and the hollowing done as for short vases. When the hollowing is finished, the job is put back between centres in the normal way while the outside is shaped, but it will now be necessary to put a plug in the open end.

There are two other home made chucks which are worth knowing about, one being a hollow wooden chuck with a cotter pin, on the same principle as the one which holds a bicycle pedal crank in place, Fig. 11, and the other a hollow wooden chuck with slits in it as shown, and a taper on the outside, this being tightened to the work by tapping a metal ring up the taper, Fig. 12.

Fig. 10 Home-made steady. Fit to work while it is between centres, then remove the tailstock

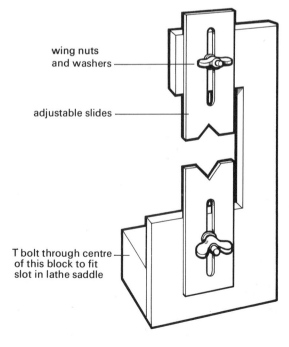

wing nuts and washers

adjustable slides

T bolt through centre of this block to fit slot in lathe saddle

114

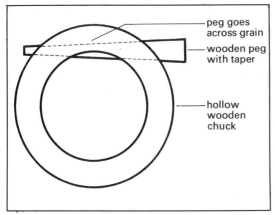

Fig. 11

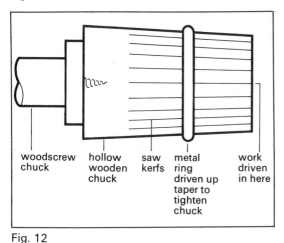

| woodscrew chuck | hollow wooden chuck | saw kerfs | metal ring driven up taper to tighten chuck | work driven in here |

Fig. 12

Fig. 13

Before leaving this chapter, a few words on the subject of lamp fittings may be helpful. Some of the brass fittings designed to carry the bulb holder have a flange with holes for small screws. There are two objections to this type, the main one being that it is not very strong, since screws do not hold well in end grain, and they are likely to be pulled out if the lamp is knocked over. The other objection is that, to make a neat job, the flange ought to be recessed into the lamp, which to my mind is unnecessary work.

The type I prefer is shown in the centre of Fig. 13, having a $\frac{3}{8}$in. (9·5mm.) Whitworth thread to go into the lamp stem, and a fine thread on the upper part to take the bulb holder. Various suggestions have been put forward as to the best method of fitting these to the lamp, such as forcing them in with the tang of a file, or making up a special tool, but since the hole which we drill through our lamp is $\frac{5}{16}$in. (7·9mm.), the best way is to run a $\frac{3}{8}$in. (9·5mm.) tap in, Fig. 14. Care must be taken to get the tapping done so that the bulb holder will be upright, you can see by the photograph that it can easily lean, and this would ruin a good lamp. As for getting the flex into place, there should be no trouble if the hole has been cleanly drilled. I find it best to push the flex through the base first, then help it on its way up the lamp stem with a thin rod, such as a knitting needle with the business end cut off.

Fig. 11 Collett chuck. The work is driven into a hollow chuck, and the tapered cotter engages with flat on work

Fig. 12 Hollow wooden chuck with slits

Fig. 13 Three types of brass fitting for the tops of electric lamps to carry the bulb holder. The best is the centre one

115

Now, since we have been trailing shavings all over the place, and spending far too much time in the workshop, we had better look to our laurels, and make something for the lady of the house—so why not a peppermill? These are functional and attractive, they take little wood, and are definitely not difficult to make, even if they do look a bit complicated. The mechanisms can be bought in various sizes, but the one I have is $5\frac{1}{2}$in. (139·7mm.) long. For this size you need a block of wood about $2\frac{1}{4}$in. (57·2mm.) square, and 7in. (177·8mm.) long. The piece I used was oak, but this is a matter of personal taste.

For part of the job you will be using a woodscrew chuck, and do make sure when you use these that the central screw is really tight, and if not, tighten it up with the little two pronged tool provided. Put the wood between centres as accurately as you can and bring it down to a cylinder with the roughing gouge, Fig. 15. The tailstock end will be the base of the article, so it should be made a little concave, with the parting tool or the point of a skew, Fig. 16, cutting, not scraping! The other end should have been cut dead square, but if not it can now be trued up.

Now measure 4in. (101·6mm.) along from the tailstock end and mark off, Fig. 17. This gives the

Fig. 14 A $\frac{3}{8}$in. [9·5mm.] Whitworth tap being used in a lamp to take the brass fitting

Fig. 15 Running the blank down to a cylinder for making a pepper mill. Note how roughing gouge is held

Fig. 16 The base of the article is made slightly concave with the long corner of a skew

116

correct length for the body of the mill, so you now part off on the left of the line, easing back the tail-stock pressure very slightly so that the work will not collapse and jam the tool. With a 1 in. (25·4mm.) drill, bore ⅝in. (15·9mm.) into the bottom of the body section, Fig. 18, either in the lathe or on a drill press. This hole will accept the female part of the grinding mechanism, Fig. 19, the tabular piece with notches on its lower edge. The drill is now changed for a ¾in. (19·1mm.) one, and the boring continues for a further ½in. (12·7mm.). This leaves a step to locate the tubular part. Now we can drill in from the other end with a 1¼in. (31·8mm.) drill to meet the other holes. When this part of the job has been completed, a tapered plug is fitted to each end of the job, the work put back between centres, and trued up with a sharp gouge. A flange to take the lid can now be cut with the parting tool, Fig. 20.

The other section of the original piece of wood is now mounted on a woodscrew chuck, the face made a little concave, and a rebate cut to take the flange on the body part, but this must be done with care. After this has been done, a ⅛in. (3·2mm.) drill is passed through the centre of the lid section, almost as far as the woodscrew point. When the fit is good enough, the whole job is put between centres to be shaped and polished, but remember

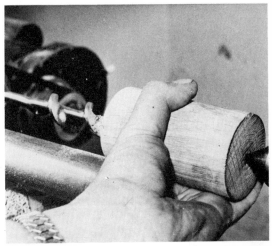

Fig. 18 Boring ⅝in. [15·9mm.] deep into the bottom of the body section with a 1in. [25·4mm.] drill

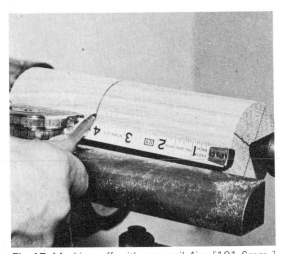

Fig. 17 Marking off with a pencil 4in. [101·6mm.] along from the end of the blank before parting through to separate cap and body

Fig. 19 The grinding mechanism shown in detail

Fig. 20 Cutting the flange on the mill body to take the lid

Fig. 22 The small metal disc has been fitted inside the lid. Note the square hole which turns the shaft when the top is revolved

Fig. 21 Two peppermills completed

when you are shaping that you cannot go in deep where the two sections meet. The final length of the cap should be such that the threaded part of the central metal rod will protrude from it when it is in place, so that the little knurled retaining nut can be fitted, Fig. 21. After the cap has been taken from the lathe, complete the drilling of the $\frac{1}{8}$in. (3·2mm.) hole, and fit the little circular metal disc centrally over this on the inner face with strong adhesive or tiny brads, Fig. 22. The little metal strip is now fitted across the bottom, recessing it in so that it will not make the mill unstable, Fig. 23, and in go the peppercorns.

Fig. 23 A small metal strip is fitted across the base

Chapter thirteen

The question of how to get a really professional finish on turned work is quite a worry to the amateur turner, and very much so in the early stages. I receive a lot of letters about this, and I cannot help feeling it might not be such a bother if people were not in so much of a hurry, for the essence of the matter is that it is useless to start any kind of finishing process before the surface is ready. It must be understood clearly that the excellent finishes produced by professionals are not the result of any kind of magic or secret knowledge. The methods they employ are really quite basic, though some have fancy mixtures of waxes and so forth by which they swear. If you just want to amuse yourself, and make something which looks fairly reasonable, then you can skip light-heartedly through the job, use abrasive paper until you are happy, and finally apply some polish or varnish. If, however, you want a finish which is as near perfect as it can be, then you must do two things.

Firstly, the job must be taken slowly, and especially so towards the end, and when the shaping is finished the lathe must be stopped, and the surface of the wood examined in an extremely critical manner. All the final cuts must be light, and done with freshly sharpened tools.

Secondly, once you are satisfied that the work is really free from blemishes, and as smooth as the tools can make it, the abrasive paper can be used. Keep it moving from side to side all the time, or it will form scratches round the work, and these will be visible through the finish. Sandpaper, glass-paper, garnet paper, or what have you, is not such a great asset to the woodturner as some think—in fact if not used properly it can be a menace. Any conception of abrasive paper as a means of correcting faulty turning is entirely wrong, all faults apparent in the work must be removed with sharp tools before the paper is used. Quite apart from anything else, great clouds of dust created by abrasives are most objectionable. Another point which is not always appreciated is that all cutting must be finished before the abrasive paper is used, since such material will leave particles of abrasive in the wood, and the tools will quickly be blunted if they are applied to it again.

Fig. 1 Two lamps turned from deal. These can be polished or sprayed with polyurethane

Different timbers have differing characteristics, which is something one learns about as the years go by, so one's finishing methods have to be modified accordingly, which to my mind is one of the things which make woodturning such a fascinating craft. The best woods for turning are the ones which suit the user, so try them all, and decide for yourself what suits you best. A friend of mine does most of his work in oak, which I am not too keen on. He, of course, has adapted all his methods to it over the years, and the results are first class. Others may prefer softer timbers, imported woods with rich colours and exotic fragrances, or even the much underestimated deal, which I love to turn, Fig. I.

In some timbers one can cut deep and hard, but others must be treated with more respect, or their fibres will be torn, and much careful treatment will be needed before any finish can be applied. I realise that I am to some extent going back over points raised previously, but they are important, and essential to good finishing.

No man who is seriously interested in mastering the craft can afford to blame the wood when things do not go right. He must remind himself that someone, somewhere, could probably make a good job of it, and that between putting the blank in the lathe, and inspecting the finished surface, he has either done things wrong or failed to do them right—which is not necessarily the same thing.

The problems inherent in spindle work are not as bad as those in faceplate turning, and I well remember how much frustration I experienced in my early days in trying to eliminate roughness on end grain, particularly with bowls. It would disappear in one place only to pop up in another, or it would be almost gone, and then come back in all its glory with my final careful cut!

Sometimes the outside would respond to treatment, but nothing would induce the inside to do the same, or the other way round. I will not enumerate all the things I tried, because the majority did not work, but I assure the student that these troubles can be overcome, with due persistence. The two best answers lie in scraping against the fibres with a sharp edge, and in taking very light cuts with a sharp gouge well over on its side, which is the real key, but the gouge must be cutting.

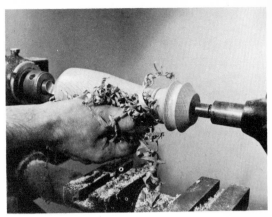

Fig. 2 A thorough burnishing is a great help in getting a good finish

In spindle work, without doubt, the biggest trouble getting a good finish on the work is ribbing. Sometimes one cannot get rid of this altogether, and has to make the best of a bad job. Another annoying thing to the turner, having gone to great lengths to learn how to handle a skew chisel for smoothing cuts, is to discover that on some woods it plucks the fibres out, leaving the surface rough, no matter how sharp it may be. Here one sometimes has to revert to a gouge, because the cutting action is different, and on that particular piece of wood it gives a better finish.

So, assuming that diligent practice has brought the turner to a fair degree of proficiency, and that he has turned some article as best he can, he must inspect it, and be utterly ruthless in his appraisal. It is either right or wrong, there is no halfway mark, and all faults must be rectified now. Sanding is done with the paper under the work, going from a medium down to a very fine grade. Some turners finish off with some fine wire wool, but this is not essential. A final burnish with a handful of shavings will help, Fig. 2, and the purist will wet the wood and allow it to dry, giving it a final fine sanding to smooth the grain which has been raised. The burnishing has a beneficial effect, but care must be taken to see that no sharp object is picked up with the shavings, and that they are not pressed too hard near thin edges, or the work will be burned. There should now be a near perfect finish on the wood, ready for the application of waxes, polishes, or whatever is to be used.

I find beeswax useful as a grain filler, but I do not polish with it as I consider it too soft. It can be applied to open grained wood as a block, following up with a pad of rag pressed on hard, so that the wax is melted and driven into the wood. This fills the grain and forms a base for the polish, which would otherwise be absorbed too easily. Beeswax can be bought in its refined form, which is creamy white in colour, or as cobbler's wax, which is dark brown, and cheaper. Some like to mix beeswax and turpentine to make a polish, which strikes me as a messy business, and I prefer to appropriate the household furniture wax from the cupboard.

Sanding sealer can be a great help on open grained woods, being applied liberally with a rag or brush across the grain, and wiped over when dry. A light sanding is then needed, with very fine paper.

A most useful polish for lathe work is the friction type, of which there are two varieties, white or brown. The white is the one I use, and an excellent finish can be obtained with it after a little practice. I find it best to coat the job liberally with this while the lathe is switched off, allow it to dry, sand with fine paper, and then build up a high gloss on the wood with the lathe running, applying the polish very sparingly with some cotton wool inside a piece of rag.

Carnauba wax is a popular medium among amateurs, because it produces a high gloss quickly, and is relatively cheap. Correct application and polishing take some getting used to. The finish it gives can be very good, but it is best avoided for articles which are likely to get a lot of handling, since it is anything but permanent. It can be applied in the same way as beeswax, aiming for a thin, even coat all over, or it can be broken up and applied inside a rag, in which case the frictional heat will bring it through on to the wood. Once applied it can be polished with a clean dry rag, but the pressure has to be exactly right. Too much pressure will melt it, and bring it up in dirty rings round the work, while too little will cause it to turn a whitish colour, and lack the high gloss we are aiming for.

For the article which is really important, and required to stand the test of time, polyurethane is the thing. It takes time to apply properly, and has to be flatted by hand between coats, but a very high gloss can be achieved, especially if the final coat is thinned. If you prefer, you can cut the last coat back with fine wire wool, to give that matt Scandinavian effect which has become so popular.

Well, there it is, I have finished and I am sorry, for I must have left a good deal unsaid, but I feel that if the instructions in this book are followed carefully, the results will be pleasing to the student, and I can only hope that he will find the deep pleasure and satisfaction that I have found in this ancient craft of woodturning.

Design Section

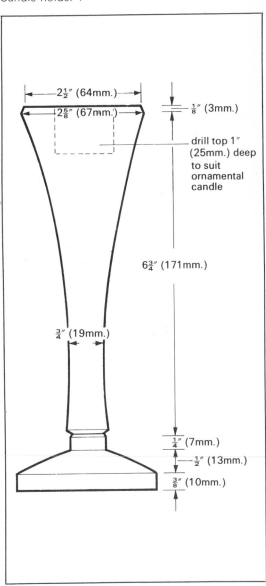

Candle holder 1

2½" (64mm.)

2⅝" (67mm.)

⅛" (3mm.)

drill top 1"
(25mm.) deep
to suit
ornamental
candle

6¾" (171mm.)

¾" (19mm.)

¼" (7mm.)

½" (13mm.)

⅜" (10mm.)

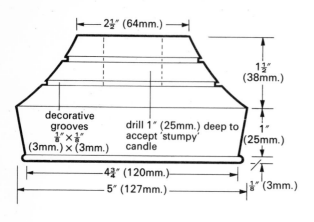

Candle holder 2—for modern, fat, coloured candles

2½″ (64mm.)

1½″ (38mm.)

decorative grooves
⅛″ × ⅛″
(3mm.) × (3mm.)

drill 1″ (25mm.) deep to accept 'stumpy' candle

1″ (25mm.)

4¾″ (120mm.)

5″ (127mm.)

⅛″ (3mm.)

Candle holder 3—in afrormosia

2″ (51mm.)

drill 1″ (25mm.) deep to suit candle

3½″ (89mm.)

½″ (13mm.)

⅜″ (10mm.)

1½″ (38mm.)

⅝″ (16mm.)

3″ (76mm.)

Three designs for table lamps

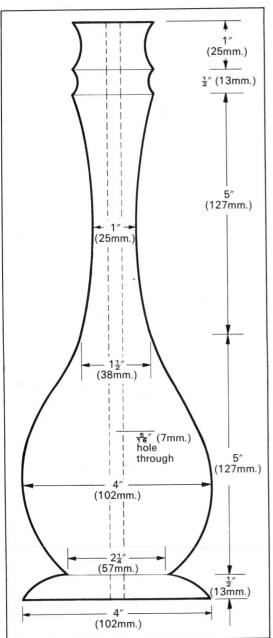

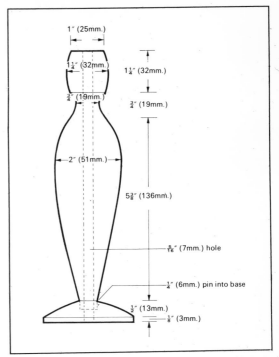

1″ (25mm.)

1¼″ (32mm.)   1¼″ (32mm.)

¾″ (19mm.)   ¾″ (19mm.)

2″ (51mm.)

5⅜″ (136mm.)

5/16″ (7mm.) hole

¼″ (6mm.) pin into base

½″ (13mm.)

⅛″ (3mm.)

1″
(25mm.)

½″ (13mm.)

5″
(127mm.)

1″
(25mm.)

1½″
(38mm.)

5/16″ (7mm.)
hole
through

5″
(127mm.)

4″
(102mm.)

2¼″
(57mm.)

½″
(13mm.)

4″
(102mm.)

Right: An exercise in sphere turning—all holes must be drilled radially

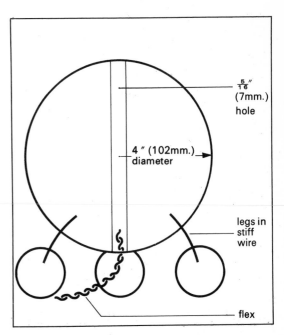

5/16″
(7mm.)
hole

4″ (102mm.)
diameter

legs in
stiff
wire

flex

125

Match barrels

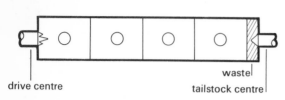

drive centre   waste
tailstock centre

Fig. 1 A 3in. (76mm.) square of ash marked out and drilled ready for turning with 1in. (25mm.) holes 1in. (25mm.) deep. Turn to a cylinder and run parting tool in on lines. Leave about 1in. (25mm.) at centre

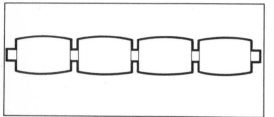

Fig. 2 Turn barrels to shape with skew chisel used on top of work. Burn on black bands with tang of file levered between work and tool rest. Part off on bandsaw or by hand, smooth ends with abrasive

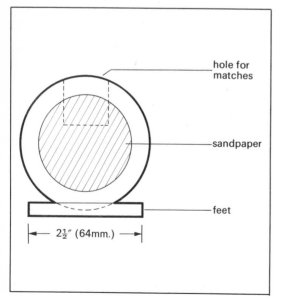

hole for matches

sandpaper

feet

2½″ (64mm.)

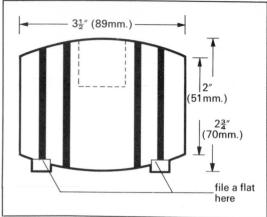

3½″ (89mm.)

2″ (51mm.)

2¾″ (70mm.)

file a flat here

A block has been marked in sections, the centre of each section found, and a 1in. by 1in. (25mm. by 25mm.) hole drilled. Here the block is securely mounted in the lathe ready for turning

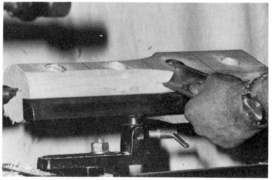

B Big half round roughing gouge in use bringing the work to a cylinder. Note the angle at which the tool is held

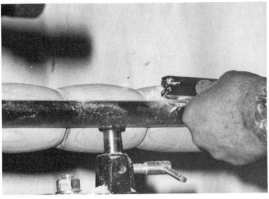

C Parting tool cuts have been made to separate the barrel sections, leaving enough wood to keep the work steady. Here the shaping is being done with a 2in. skew chisel

F Barrels have been separated in a few moments on the bandsaw

D Burning on the 'hoops'. This is done by forcing the tang of a file or old scraper between work and rest and applying leverage

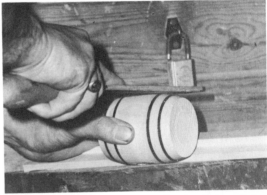

G Filing two flats in readiness for the fitting of the feet. This can be done better with the aid of some simple form of jig

E left The barrels turned and marked, and ready to be separated

Index